The CONSUMER BANKING
Regulatory Handbook

1998–1999 Edition

Sharpe Professional

An imprint of M.E. Sharpe, INC.

Copyright © PricewaterhouseCoopers, 1999

All rights reserved. No part of this book may be reproduced in any form without written permission from the publisher, M. E. Sharpe, Inc., 80 Business Park Drive, Armonk, New York 10504

This publication is designed to provide accurate and authoritative information in regard to the subject matter covered. It is sold with the understanding that the publisher is not engaged in rendering legal, accounting, or other professional service. If legal advice or other expert assistance is required, the services of a competent professional person should be sought.

—From the Declaration of Principles jointly adopted by a Committee of the American Bar Association and a Committee of Publishers and Associations

ISBN 0-7656-0267-9
ISSN 1090-2546

Printed in the United States of America

(IPC) 10 9 8 7 6 5 4 3 2 1

TABLE OF CONTENTS

	Introduction	3
I.	Adjustable Rate Mortgage Rules	7
II.	Bank Enterprise Act	11
III.	Bank Secrecy Act	17
IV.	Community Reinvestment Act	45
V.	Consumer Leasing Act	57
VI.	Credit Practices Rules	65
VII.	Deposit Insurance	71
VIII.	Electronic Fund Transfer Act	79
IX.	Equal Credit Opportunity Act	89
X.	Equal Employment Opportunity Act	105
XI.	Expedited Funds Availability Act	111
XII.	Fair Credit Reporting Act	123
XIII.	Fair Debt Collection Practices Act	129
XIV.	Fair Housing Act	135
XV.	Flood Disaster Protection Act	143
XVI.	Home Mortgage Disclosure Act	153
XVII.	Homeownership Counseling	159
XVIII.	Interest on Deposits	163
XIX.	Real Estate Settlement Procedures Act	169
XX.	Right to Financial Privacy Act	183
XXI.	Truth in Lending Act	189
XXII.	Truth in Savings Act	223
	Index	233

The CONSUMER BANKING
Regulatory Handbook

Introduction

The Consumer Banking Regulatory Handbook

The Regulatory Advisory Services practice of **PricewaterhouseCoopers** has prepared *The Consumer Banking Regulatory Handbook* to provide the firm and its clients, with a summary of the major federal laws and regulations enforced through regulatory compliance examinations. Most of these laws have been designed to protect consumers.

The Regulatory Handbook Series

This *Handbook* is one in a series of Handbooks that Regulatory Advisory Services has written to give financial institutions and their advisers current information on financial institution regulatory and supervisory policies and procedures.

The Consumer Banking Regulatory Handbook summarizes subjects that bank examiners review in a regulatory compliance examination. Other books in the series emphasize other types of subjects reviewed in financial institution examinations: *The Commercial Banking Regulatory Handbook* focuses on safety and soundness examination and *The Trust Regulatory Handbook* concentrates on trust examination. Two other books in the series focus on specialized subjects that frequently pose serious compliance problems to financial institutions. These include regulatory reporting and securities activities. *The Regulatory Risk Management Handbook*, the newest book in the series, adds general information designed to help financial institutions and their advisers better understand the overall scheme of bank supervision as regulators increasingly shift to risk management as a basis for examinations. The seventh book of the series, *The Compliance Link*, is a comprehensive cross-index volume.

The 90 Percent Solution

We have written this *Handbook* and others in the series intending to give readers a plain language answer to 90 percent of the compliance problems they may encounter. We have specifically avoided trying to answer all possible compliance questions. Thus, we emphasize concepts and regulatory risk management advice over detailed explanations of the law and regulations.

Our principal goal is to familiarize a reader with the requirements of a law or regulation. We recognize that someone may want more information on a subject and, therefore, we include in each section a reference to the laws, regulations, and regulatory policies on the subject.

Highlights of the 1998 - 99 Edition

Because of the frequency with which these laws and regulations are changed or new ones added, we revise this *Handbook* annually. We have made changes in almost all sections of the *Handbook*. The most significant changes for this edition are:

- *Bank Secrecy Act*–Amendments eliminate the requirement to report transactions in currency in excess of $10,000 between depository institutions and certain classes of "exempt" persons;

- *Expedited Funds Availability Act*–Amendments address the treatment of deposits received at contractual branches and provide more flexibility for hold notices under emergency conditions;

- *Home Mortgage Disclosure Act*–Amendments set the asset exemption threshold for depository institutions at $28 million;

- *Truth in Lending Act*–Amendments provide guidance on the treatment of fees paid in connection with mortgage loans and address new accuracy tolerances in finance charge disclosures.

Caution

Readers should be cautioned that, although we have highlighted the key legal requirements of the various consumer laws, the area remains quite complex, with many technical requirements and frequent new agency interpretations. Therefore, use the *Handbook* as only one resource in addition to reviewing the actual law or regulation or seeking additional counsel or advice.

The Compliance Examination

Over the past several years, each of the financial regulatory agencies — the OCC, FRB, FDIC, and OTS — has organized and trained specialized examination teams whose sole mission is to examine financial institutions for compliance with the laws and regulations described in this *Handbook*. This examination process is independent from the traditional safety and soundness exam. Specially trained examiners conduct the examination and is-

Introduction 5

sue a separate consumer compliance exam report to the institution's board of directors.

The primary purpose of the regulatory consumer compliance exam is to evaluate the overall quality and effectiveness of the institution's consumer compliance program. As part of this process, examiners also will test a sampling of transactions in those areas deemed to have inadequate or deficient compliance programs or internal review procedures. In all cases, the examination will include a specific review of certain sensitive areas such as the Bank Secrecy Act, Nondiscrimination Laws, CRA, and other areas of current concern.

PwC Regulatory Advisory Services

The **PricewaterhouseCoopers** Regulatory Advisory Services practice in Washington, D.C., consists of former senior bank regulators, attorneys, and bankers who advise their clients on a broad range of U.S. bank regulatory and business issues. The group is prepared to assist any financial institution in developing an effective compliance program or in evaluating its existing compliance program. Regulatory Advisory Services is also prepared to review an institution's policies and procedures in a particular area as well as conduct on-site examinations to assist the institution in evaluating its level of compliance or in preparing for a regulatory exam.

If you would like additional information about the material contained in this *Handbook,* or about the compliance services offered by **PricewaterhouseCoopers** Regulatory Advisory Services, please call:

Paul G. Nelson	(202) 414-4331
C. Westbrook Murphy	(202) 414-4301
Gary M. Welsh	(202) 414-4311
Jeffrey P. Lavine	(202) 414-4320
David R. Sapin	(202) 414-4321
Paul Allan Schott	(202) 822-4272
Andrea Conte	(202) 414-4308

I. Adjustable Rate Mortgage Rules

Introduction and Purpose 8

ARM Special Information Booklet 8

ARM Initial Disclosure Information 8

ARM Adjustment Requirements 9

ARM Adjustment Notices 10

ARM Maximum Interest Rates 10

ARM Rate Formula or Index 10

References 10

8 Consumer Banking Regulatory Handbook

Introduction and Purpose

Beginning in the early 1980s, the federal financial regulatory agencies began issuing regulations governing the ability of financial institutions to offer adjustable rate mortgages (ARMs). The focus of the regulations was to assure that the borrower was provided with adequate information about the terms and conditions of the loan. In an effort to achieve greater uniformity among the ARM regulations of the various agencies, the FFIEC recommended uniform disclosures for ARMs in 1986. As a result, the current disclosure requirements of the financial regulatory agencies are now substantially the same.

ARM Special Information Booklet

A financial institution must supply a copy of the publication *Consumer Handbook on Adjustable Rate Mortgages* (or a suitable substitute) to each loan applicant at the earliest of either receiving the application or receiving a non-refundable fee as payment. This includes applications that are taken over the phone.

ARM Initial Disclosure Information

When receiving the special information booklet, the potential borrower must also be given a disclosure statement for each adjustable rate product in which he or she has expressed an interest.

Each disclosure statement must include:

1. A statement that the interest rate, payment, or term of the loan may change;

2. The index or formula that will be used in making adjustments;

3. At least one independent, readily available source for the customer to locate the index rate;

4. An explanation of how the interest rate and payments will be determined;

5. An explanation of how the index is adjusted;

6. Instructions for the consumer to inquire about current margin value and interest rate;

7. A statement on whether the interest rate will be discounted and, if so, instructions for the customer to inquire about the amount of the discount;

8. The frequency of interest rate and payment changes;

9. Any rules relating to changes in the index, interest rate, payment amount, and outstanding loan balance including, for example, an explanation of interest rate or payment limitations, negative amortization, and interest rate carryover. Loans with more than one way to trigger negative amortization are separate variable-rate loan programs, and thus require separate disclosures to the extent that they vary from each other;

10. A 15-year historical example, based on a $10,000 loan, showing all significant payment terms including the interest and payment changes that would have occurred under the terms of that adjustable rate program. The example must be updated each year to reflect data from the most recent 15-year period;

11. An explanation of how the most recent payment used in the 15-year example can be used by the consumer to calculate the payments for the loan amount;

12. The *initial* interest rate and payment and the maximum interest rate and payment for a sample $10,000 loan originated at the most recent rate stated in the 15-year example, assuming the maximum periodic increases in rates and payments;

13. The fact that the loan contains a demand feature;

14. The type of information that will be included in notices of adjustments;

15. The timing of adjustment notices; and

16. A statement that disclosure forms are available for an association's other variable-rate products.

ARM Adjustment Requirements

Interest rate adjustments must correspond directly with the movement of an index, a formula, or a schedule set forth in the loan contract that specifies the amount of the increase and the time at which it may be made.

Payment and loan balance adjustments that do not reflect an adjustment in the interest rate may be made only if:

1. They reflect a change in a national or regional index available to the borrower outside the control of the institution that measures the rate of inflation or changes in consumer disposable income; or

2. In the case of a payment adjustment, the adjustment reflects a change in the loan balance or is made based on a formula or schedule set forth in the loan contract.

10 Consumer Banking Regulatory Handbook

ARM Adjustment Notices

Once the loan has been made, notice must be given to the borrower whenever an adjustment is made to the borrower's interest rate or payment amount.

Notice of all *interest rate* changes without a payment change must be made to the borrower at least *once* a year.

Notice of all *payment changes* must be delivered or mailed to the borrower between *25 and 120 calendar days before the due date* of the new payment level.

A notice of a change in interest rates or payments must include:

1. The current and prior interest rates;
2. The index values upon which the current and prior interest rates are based;
3. The extent to which an association has forgone any increase in the interest rate;
4. The contractual effects of the adjustment, including the payment due after the adjustment and statement of the loan balance; and
5. The amount of payment necessary to fully amortize the loan at the new interest rate over the remainder of the loan term if that amount is different from the new payment that has resulted from the adjustment.

ARM Maximum Interest Rates

A financial institution must state in every ARM note the maximum interest rate that may be imposed during the term of the loan. The Truth in Lending regulations require this disclosure for both open-end and closed-end loans.

ARM Rate Formula or Index

Once selected, the formula or index rate value specified on the original note must be used for the duration of the loan.

References

Laws:

15 U.S.C. 1601 et seq.

Regulations:

12 CFR Part 34 (OCC)
12 CFR 226.19(b), 226.20(c), and 226.30 (Reg Z) (FRB)
12 CFR 545.33(c) and 563.99 (OTS)

II. Bank Enterprise Act

Introduction and Purpose 12

Lifeline Accounts 12

Banking in Distressed Communities 13

Community Development Financial Institutions Fund 14

References 16

**Introduction
and Purpose**

The Bank Enterprise Act of 1991 ("BEA") encourages banks — through enticement of lower FDIC assessments — to provide two services to low- and moderate-income individuals. These services are:

- Lifeline checking accounts; and

- Increased loans and deposits in distressed communities.

The BEA is not yet effective. The Act provides that it will not take effect until Congress specifically appropriates funds to compensate the FDIC for any losses that may result from application of the Act.

Lifeline Accounts

A "lifeline account" is a checking or NOW account with a balance under $1,000 and minimum restrictions and service fees. The deposit insurance assessment rate for these lifeline accounts will be 50 percent of the institution's maximum BIF or SAIF assessment rate.

The BEA specifies that the Federal Reserve Board and the FDIC should establish the minimum parameters for lifeline account qualification. Among the criteria the Board and the FDIC must consider are:

- Whether the account is available for basic transaction services for balances of less than $1,000;

- Whether the minimal fees are charged for routine transactions;

- Whether there are minimal opening and account balance requirements;

- Whether checks are permitted;

- Whether monthly statements are available;

- Whether depositors have access to tellers for account transactions;

- Whether there are any account prerequisites that discriminate against low-income individuals; and

- Whether any other account relationships are required in order to open up the account.

Banking in Distressed Communities

The BEA also established a program to provide reduced semiannual FDIC assessment credit for those institutions that engage in "qualifying activities" for the improvement of "distressed communities."

The BEA specifies certain "qualifying activities" that may make institutions eligible for the reduced assessments. In lending, qualifying activities include increases in the amount of new loan origination to:

- Low- or moderate-income persons in "distressed communities"; or

- Enterprises integrally involved in such communities.

These loans and enterprises must be deemed as "qualified" by the Community Enterprise Assessment Credit Board ("CEACB"). The BEA is very specific in its definition of "qualified loans," and generally limits them to federally assisted or guaranteed loans and to mortgages targeted at low- and moderate-income persons.

Qualifying activities also include:

- Increases in deposits from persons domiciled in distressed communities;

- Deposits made at branches located in the distressed community;

- Loans made within that community; and

- Any increase during the period in new equity investments in community development financial institutions.

Definition of a Distressed Community

Subject to agency approval, an institution may designate a community as "distressed" if it meets both the eligibility and minimum area requirements. The minimum area that may be certified as a distressed community is measured by population within a contiguous boundary. To qualify, the community must have a population of at least 4,000 for communities within a metropolitan statistical area with a population of 50,000 or more, or 1,000 for all other communities.

The distressed community eligibility requirement is met by satisfying the following criteria:

- **Poverty.** At least 30 percent of the residents of the area have incomes that are less than the national poverty level; and

- **Unemployment.** The community unemployment rate is at least 150 percent of the national average.

Deposit Insurance Assessment Credit

The semiannual assessment credit available on qualifying activities is 5 percent of the institution's total semiannual assessment. If the institution qualifies as a "community development organization" a rigorous test must be met under the BEA in order to qualify — then the credit is increased to 15 percent of the total semiannual assessment. The FDIC may increase the assessment credit available for qualifying deposit activity, but the percentage established for an institution qualifying as a "community development organization" must be at least three times greater than the percentage established for a nonqualifying institution.

Community development financial institutions also qualify for a 15 percent assessment credit.

Community Development Financial Institutions Fund

Although the BEA continues to remain ineffective, many of its objectives recently materialized in the Community Development Financial Institutions Act of 1994. Under this act, the Community Development Financial Institutions Fund (the Fund) administers programs to promote activity among financial institutions that serve distressed communities. In October 1995, the Fund established two new programs, the Community Development Financial Institutions Program (CDFI Program) and the Bank Enterprise Awards Program (BEA Program). Together, these two programs work to facilitate the flow of lending and investment capital into distressed communities and to individuals who have been unable to take full advantage of the financial services industry.

Under both programs, institutions compete through an application process to receive financial assistance from the Fund. The Fund rates and selects applicants based on their planned projects.

Eligibility Requirements

An entity is considered a community development financial institution, and is eligible for assistance from the Fund, if it:

- Has a primary mission of promoting community development;

- Serves a target market (an investment area or targeted population);

- Is a financing entity whose predominant business activity is the provision of loans or development investments;

- Provides development services;

- Maintains accountability to the target market; and

- Is a nongovernment entity.

An institution may receive assistance from either the CDFI Program or the BEA Program, but not from both.

Community Development Financial Institutions Program

Under the CDFI Program, the Fund provides financial and technical assistance to selected applicants to enhance their ability to serve designated "investment areas," "targeted populations," or both. An investment area is defined as a community that meets certain objective criteria of distress. A targeted population is defined as individuals (or a group of individuals) who are low-income persons or who lack adequate access to loans or equity investments.

The Fund requires that all applicants obtain matching funds from sources other than the federal government before they can be selected for an award. After selection, an institution must enter into an assistance agreement that requires it to achieve financial, organizational development, and community impact performance goals.

Bank Enterprise Awards Program

The BEA Program is based directly on the provisions of the Bank Enterprise Act. The Fund evaluates applicants by the value of their proposed increases in "qualifying activities." Qualifying activities are both eligible development activities (including loans and financial services) and equity investments. The Fund awards selected applicants that:

- Invest in community development financial institutions;

- Increase lending activities within distressed communities; or

- Increase the provision of certain services and assistance.

Distressed communities must meet the minimum poverty and unemployment criteria that were established in the Bank Enterprise Act. Only after successful completion of the qualifying activities do the program participants receive monies.

References

Laws:

    12 U.S.C. 1834

Regulations:

    12 CFR 1805 and 1806

III. Bank Secrecy Act

Introduction and Purpose		19
I.	Currency Transaction Report	19
	CTR Filing	20
	CTR Form	20
	Aggregation of Multiple Transactions	21
II.	CTR Exemptions	21
	General Exemptions	24
	Unilateral Exemptions	24
	Special Exemptions	25
	Customer Exemption Statement	25
	Exempt Customer List	26
III.	Monetary Instruments Transaction Records	27
	Required Information	27
IV.	Payable Through Accounts	28
V.	Suspicious Transactions	30
VI.	Structuring	30

18 Consumer Banking Regulatory Handbook

VII. Funds Transfers 31

      Payment Order Information (The Travel Rule) 33

VIII. Know Your Customer Requirements 35

IX. Forfeiture 37

X. Transportation of Currency and Monetary Instruments ("CMIR") 37

      CMIR Filing 38

      Common Carrier Exemption 38

      Financial Institution Responsibilities 38

XI. Foreign Bank Account Reporting (FBAR) 39

XII. Compliance Program 39

      Program Elements 39

XIII. Other Recordkeeping Requirements 41

XIV. Registration of Nondepository Institutions 43

References 44

Bank Secrecy Act

Introduction and Purpose

The Bank Secrecy Act (BSA) was passed by Congress in 1970 to require financial institutions to file certain currency and monetary instrument reports and maintain certain records for possible use in criminal, tax, and regulatory proceedings. The Act was strengthened by the Money Laundering and Control Act of 1986 (MLCA), amendments to the 1986 Act passed in 1988, the Annunzio-Wylie Anti-Money Laundering Act of 1992, and the Money Laundering Suppression Act of 1994. It is implemented by regulations issued by the Treasury Department (31 CFR 103).

The original purpose of the BSA was primarily to provide a paper trail of the activities of money launderers serving the interests of drug traffickers and other elements of white collar and organized crime. These activities generate large amounts of currency, often in small bills. During the course of these activities, the cash may be exchanged for larger denominations or converted to other monetary instruments for ease of use.

Because transaction reporting and recordkeeping requirements have been successful in reducing the avenues available to money launderers, criminals have been forced to find new ways to launder money. To further limit money laundering through these new channels that criminals have developed, the federal regulatory agencies, over the past two years, have issued final rules on funds transfers, issued guidelines for protecting payable through accounts from improper or illegal use, and implemented a final rule on exemptions from CTR filing requirements. The regulators also emphasize that institutions should have in place Know Your Customer policies and procedures.

The importance of complying with the BSA cannot be overemphasized. Findings of particular violations may result in assessment of substantial criminal and civil penalties. Convictions of money laundering or certain BSA offenses may also result in termination of banking licenses.

Institutions Subject to the Bank Secrecy Act

The Bank Secrecy Act applies to all "financial institutions" located within the United States, including banks, thrifts, nonbank financial institutions such as securities brokers or dealers required to be registered with the SEC, currency exchange houses, casinos, and persons engaged in the business of transmitting funds.

I. Currency Transaction Report

A financial institution must file a Currency Transaction Report (CTR), Form 4789, each time a customer makes a deposit, withdrawal, exchange, or other transfer of more than $10,000 in currency. Currency includes coins and currency of the United States or any other country, which circulates and is used as money. It does not include bank checks or other negotiable instruments.

A CTR is required if the customer exceeds $10,000 in one cash transaction, or exceeds $10,000 in multiple cash transactions in one business day. In certain cases, transactions spread over a number of days may constitute a reportable transaction. (See Section on Structured Transactions).

A CTR may also be required for amounts less than $10,000 if the Treasury Department determines that there is an unusually high incidence of money laundering in a specific geographic area. Financial institutions subject to this determination may not disclose the existence of the order.

CTR Filing

Completed CTRs are filed by the financial institution with the IRS Data Center in Detroit, Michigan, within 15 days of the transaction date. For magnetic media filing, CTRs must be filed within 25 days of the transaction. Institutions must retain a copy of each report filed for a period of five years from the date of the report.

CTR Form

The following information is required on each CTR:

- The name, address, social security number or taxpayer identification number (TIN), and other identifying information on the individual who conducted the transaction with the financial institution, and the method used to identify the individual;

- If appropriate, the name, address, social security number or TIN, and other identifying information on the individual on whose behalf the transaction with the financial institution was conducted;

- The type of transaction, for example, currency exchange, deposit, withdrawal, wire transfer, check cashing, etc.;

- The total amount of cash in and/or cash out and date of the currency transaction;

- The name, address, federal regulatory code, and other identifying information on the financial institution where the transaction took place; and

- Additional information if multiple persons were involved in the transaction.

Aggregation of Multiple Transactions

Multiple transactions must be aggregated and treated as a single transaction if a financial institution has knowledge that the transactions were made by (or on behalf of) the same person on the same day.

Institutions are not required to purchase new computer software if their existing software cannot aggregate transactions in different accounts of the same person. However, regulators recommend that when institutions consider purchasing computer systems or software they should purchase systems that can aggregate multiple accounts.

II. CTR Exemptions

> The Treasury issued a final rule, effective January 1, 1998, which exempts transactions, in currency in excess of $10,000, between "banks" and certain classes of "exempt persons" from CTR reporting requirements.

The Money Laundering Suppression Act of 1994 (MLSA) contains mandatory and discretionary exemptions to the mandatory reporting requirements. Under this Act, the Treasury is required to devise mandatory exemptions from CTR filings and publish, at least annually, a list (by type) of exempt entities. To meet this requirement, the Treasury issued a final rule, effective January 1, 1998, which exempts transactions, in currency in excess of $10,000, between "banks" and certain classes of "exempt persons, from the CTR reporting requirement." The text below discusses exemptions under the MLSA and final rule. Coverage of current administrative exemption requirements follows the discussion of the final rule.

For the purposes of the final rule exemptions, the term "bank" is broadly defined to include most financial institutions with the exception of nonbank financial institutions (e.g., commercial banks and trust companies, private banks, credit unions, savings and loans, foreign banks, and U.S. branches and agencies of foreign banks are included). Transactions with "banks" by the following are exempt from the CTR reporting requirement:

1. *A bank*, to the extent of such bank's domestic operations;

2. *Any federal or state governmental entity*;

3. *Entities exercising governmental authority* — any entity that exercises governmental authority on behalf of the United States or any state;

4. *Listed corporations* — any corporation (to the extent of its domestic operations) listed on the New York or American Stock Exchanges (except stock listed on the American Exchange's Emerging Company Marketplace) or whose common stock has been designated as a NASDAQ National Market Security (except stock listed as a "NASDAQ Small-Cap Issue");

5. *Subsidiaries of listed corporations* - any subsidiary (to the extent of its domestic operations) of a listed corporation described in paragraph 4 that is:

- Organized under U.S. laws or of any state, and

- At least 51 percent of its common stock is owned by the listed corporation;

6. *Financial institutions:* A financial institution, other than a bank, that is an entity described in paragraphs 4 or 5 to the extent of such financial institutions domestic operations.

A bank that wishes to use the exemptions must designate as exempt each entity for which it wishes to rely on the final rule. The bank must make this designation within 30 days following the first currency transaction between a bank and an exempt entity. To designate an entity as exempt, an institution must either file a Currency Transaction Report and mark the "Designation of Exempt Person" box (line 36) or file any form specifically designated by the Financial Crimes Enforcement Network ("FinCEN"). An institution must designate an entity as exempt regardless of whether it previously treated the entity as exempt.

Determination of an Exempt Entity

An institution must take reasonable steps to assure itself that it may treat an entity as exempt. An institution may treat a governmental entity as exempt if:

- The name of the entity reasonably indicates that the customer is a governmental entity; or

- The customer is generally known in the community to be a state, tribal government, or a territory or possession of the United States, its political subdivision, or wholly owned agency.

An institution may consider an entity as exercising governmental authority on behalf of the United States, a state, or a political subdivision only if the entity's authorities include one or more of the powers to tax, to exercise the authority of eminent domain, or to police powers with respect to matters within its jurisdiction.

For corporations listed on the New York and American Stock Exchanges and the NASDAQ market, a bank may rely on:

- listings published in newspapers of general circulation;

- any commonly accepted or published stock symbol guide;

- any information contained on the Securities and Exchange Commission "Edgar" System; or

- any information contained in an Internet World Wide Web site or sites maintained by the New York Stock Exchange, the American Stock Exchange, or the NASDAQ market.

To determine whether an entity is an eligible subsidiary, a bank may rely upon:

- Any reasonably authenticated corporate officer's certificate;

- A reasonably authenticated photocopy of an Internal Revenue Service Affiliation Schedule (Form 851);

- The entity's Annual Report or Form 10-K, as filed with the Securities and Exchange Commission.

The rule applies only to the companies with a corporate charter, not to equity interests of some partnerships and business trusts that are listed on the named securities exchanges.

Limitation of Exemption

The exemption does not apply to situations in which an exempt entity is engaging in a transaction as an agent on behalf of another, beneficial owner of currency. (If the principal for whom the agent is acting is itself exempt, the exempt status of the principal is what causes the transaction to be exempt.)

Limited Safe Harbor

If an institution properly determines that a customer is exempt, the institution may not be penalized for failing to file a CTR for a currency transaction with the customer. The protection does not apply if the institution:

- Knowingly files false or incomplete information with respect to the transaction or the customer engaging in the transaction; or

- Has reason to believe at the time it grants the exemption that the customer does not meet the exemption criteria or that the transaction is not the transaction of an exempt customer.

Revocation of Exemption

An entity that is exempt continues to remain exempt until:

- FinCEN revokes the entity's exempt status;

- The corporation ceases to be listed on the applicable stock exchange; or

- The subsidiary of an exempt corporation ceases to have at least 51 percent of its common stock owned by the exempt corporation.

Institutions are not exempt from reporting suspected violations of any law or regulation or suspected criminal activity where reporting is required.

In addition to the exemptions under the final rule, the current administrative exemptions provide three types of exemptions from CTR reporting. These include:

1. *General Exemptions* - for customers whose cash transactions are automatically exempt;

2. *Unilateral Exemptions* - for customers who may be exempted at the discretion of the financial institution; and

3. *Special Exemptions* - for customers who may be exempted only with regulatory approval.

General Exemptions

The following transactions are always exempt from CTR reporting requirements:

- Transactions with Federal Reserve Banks and Federal Home Loan Banks; and

- Transactions by nonbank financial institutions with commercial banks (however, commercial banks must report the transactions with nonbank financial institutions).

The name and address of each exempt domestic financial institution must appear on the financial institution's exemption list, discussed below, but no maximum exemption amount is necessary. Federal Reserve Banks and Federal Home Loan Banks need not be listed on the exemption list.

Unilateral Exemptions

A financial institution may, at its option, exempt certain transactions of certain customers from CTR reporting requirements without seeking regulatory approval. There are three categories of unilateral exemptions:

1. *Retail Businesses*. Institutions may exempt from CTR reporting currency deposits and withdrawals by its established depositors that are retail businesses located in the U.S. Regulations define retail businesses to include those primarily engaged in providing goods to ultimate consumers who typically pay in currency. Regulations exclude certain types of businesses from this exemption, including dealerships selling most vehicles, vessels, and aircraft.

2. *Specifically Enumerated Businesses*. Regulations allow institutions to exempt from CTR reporting deposits and withdrawals by established depositors operating certain types of businesses, located in the United States, that are specified in BSA regulations. The following types of businesses are included: sports arenas, racetracks, amusement parks, bars, restaurants, hotels, licensed check-cashing services, vending machine companies, theaters, regularly scheduled passenger carriers, and public utilities.

3. *Payroll Withdrawals*. Regulations allow institutions to exempt from CTR reporting withdrawals for payroll purposes by established depositors who are U.S. residents and who operate firms that withdraw more than $10,000 to pay employees in currency.

Special Exemptions

A financial institution may apply to the Commissioner of Internal Revenue for a special exemption when the institution believes that circumstances warrant an exemption from CTR reporting for a customer, but no unilateral exemption is available.

Customer Exemption Statement

For each customer that an institution designates as exempt under the administrative exemption requirements (other than a domestic bank, a Federal Reserve Bank, or a Federal Home Loan Bank), BSA regulations require an institution to prepare a written statement describing the conduct of the customer's business and why the customer is qualified for an exemption from CTR reporting. The statement must be signed by the customer and a bank official.

The IRS has published a Model Customer Exemption Statement. The statement includes two parts: Part I is completed and signed by the customer, and Part II is completed by the financial institution requesting the exemption.

The institution must retain the exemption statement as long as the customer is on the exempt list, and for five years following the removal of the customer from the institution's exempt list. If the financial institution learns that any of the information on the exemption statement has changed, it should also obtain a new statement, and update the exempt customer list.

Exempt Customer List

Institutions must maintain a centralized list of all exempt customers. A properly completed exemption list should include:

- Names and addresses of all exempt domestic banks;

- Name, address, taxpayer identification number, and account number of each exempt customer;

- Description of customer's business;

- Statements as to whether the exemption covers deposits, withdrawals, or both;

- Whether the exemption is limited to certain types of deposits and withdrawals (e.g., withdrawals for payroll purposes, deposits on Mondays or after a holiday weekend);

- Dollar limits for each type of exemption, as well as the reason for the exemption (specific limits are not required for exempt customers that are domestic banks); and

- The date each exemption was granted and the dates of any changes in the exempted amounts.

> Management is responsible for reviewing transactions with exempt customers to assure the continued suitability of their exemptions. The Treasury Department recommends that institutions complete an exempt customer list review at least annually, and preferably once every six months.

Management is responsible for reviewing transactions with exempt customers to assure the continued suitability of their exemptions. The Treasury Department recommends that financial institutions complete an exempt customer list review at least annually, and preferably once every six months. This review should include contact with the customer and observation of account activity to determine whether there are any changes in the customer's situation that affect the appropriateness of the exemption. Exemptions should be limited or terminated as necessary.

III. Monetary Instruments Transaction Records

A financial institution must verify and record information relating to the identity of the purchaser of monetary instruments in exchange for currency in amounts between $3,000 and $10,000. For this purpose, "monetary instrument" is defined as a bank check, cashier's check, traveler's check, or money order. The institution must maintain identifying information as well as information about the transaction. The records must be made available to Treasury upon request.

Multiple purchases during the same business day, by or on behalf of the same person, and totaling $3,000 or more, must be recorded if any employee, director, officer, or partner of the financial institution has knowledge that these purchases have occurred. If multiple purchases during the same business day aggregate to $10,000 or more, log entries and a CTR would be required. A single monetary instrument purchased for cash in excess of $10,000 would require filing a CTR but not a log entry.

Required Information

The institution must verify that the individual is a deposit accountholder or verify the individual's identity.

If the purchaser has a deposit account with the institution, then at a minimum, the institution must record and maintain the following information:

1. Name of the purchaser;
2. Date of purchase;
3. Type(s) of instrument(s) purchased;
4. Serial number(s) of each of the instrument(s) purchased; and
5. Dollar amount(s) of each of the instrument(s) purchased in currency.

If the purchaser does not have a deposit account with the institution, the institution must verify the purchaser's name and address by examining a document normally acceptable as identification when cashing checks for nondepositors. At a minimum, the institution must record and maintain the following information.

1. Name and address of the purchaser;
2. Social security or alien identification number of the purchaser;

3. Date of birth of purchaser;
4. Date of purchase;
5. Type(s) of instrument(s) purchased;
6. Serial number(s) of each of the instrument(s) purchased;
7. Dollar amount(s) of each of the instrument(s) purchased; and
8. Method of verifying the identity of the purchaser and specific identifying information.

IV. Payable Through Accounts

The federal regulatory agencies have developed guidelines to assist financial institutions in preventing improper or illegal use of "payable through accounts" (PTA). The information provided there addresses only those areas of concern to the regulators. It does not cover the typical payable through accounts used by credit unions and investment companies.

Payable through, or pass-through, accounts are checking accounts offered by financial institutions in the United States to foreign banks that are not licensed to conduct business in the United States. Under this PTA arrangement, a U.S. bank, Edge corporation, or the U.S. branch or agency of a foreign bank ("U.S. banking entities") opens a master checking account in the name of a foreign bank.

The foreign bank subsequently divides the master account into "subaccounts," each in the name of one of the foreign bank's customers. The foreign bank extends signature authority on its master account to its own customers. The number of subaccounts permitted under this arrangement is virtually unlimited.

Deposits into the master account may flow through the foreign bank, which pools them for daily transfer to the U.S. banking entity, or the funds may flow directly to the U.S. banking entity for credit to the master account, with further credit to the subaccount. Checks encoded with the foreign bank's account number, along with a numeric code to identify the subaccount, provide subaccount holders with access to the U.S. payments system. Thus, the PTA mechanism permits the foreign bank operating outside the United States to offer its customers, the subaccount holders, U.S. dollar–denominated checks and ancillary services, which may include the ability to receive wire transfers and deposits into the subaccounts and to cash checks.

These accounts generally have a large number of foreign signatories (subaccount holders) who were not likely subject to the same type of information and verification requirements as are individuals and businesses that open accounts in the United States. For this reason, and because a U.S. institution may not have the ability independently to obtain or verify the information provided by the signatories, the regulatory agencies have determined that payable through accounts are particularly susceptible to the risk of money laundering.

Policies and Procedures

U.S. institutions must have policies and procedures designed to guard against possible improper or illegal use of payable through accounts by foreign banks and their customers. Each U.S. institution offering payable through accounts to foreign banks must be able to identify the ultimate users of the account by obtaining or having the ability to obtain, in the United States, the same type of information about the signatories as the institution obtains for its domestic customers.

Appropriate methods for meeting this requirement include:

- Reviewing the foreign bank's own procedures for identifying and monitoring subaccount holders; and

- Reviewing the requirements placed on the foreign bank by its home country supervisor for identifying and monitoring the transactions of the foreign bank's own customers.

Additionally, U.S. institutions should have procedures to monitor activities in foreign banks' payable through accounts and to report suspicious or unusual activity as required by suspicious activities regulations.

Adequate Information Unavailable

Under agency guidelines, a U.S. institution must be able to:

- Obtain, in the United States, sufficient information about the signatories;

- Rely on the foreign bank's home country supervisory requirements;

- Ensure that its payable through accounts are not being used for money laundering or other illicit purposes.

If the U.S. institution cannot meet one of these conditions, the agencies recommend that the institution terminate the payable through arrangement with the foreign bank as soon as possible.

V. Suspicious Transactions

Financial institutions are required to report suspicious transactions even if they do not exceed $10,000. Suspicious transactions for BSA purposes are defined as those that indicate possible money laundering or attempts to evade BSA requirements. Such transactions should be reported even when there is no substantial basis for identifying a possible suspect or group of suspects.

Examples of customer activities that might be considered suspicious are:

- Taking back a portion of the currency or reducing a withdrawal to place the transaction below the reporting/recording threshold; and

- Repeated below-threshold transactions on consecutive or near consecutive days (structuring).

Institutions must report suspicious transactions on the Suspicious Activity Report ("SAR"). (See the Criminal and Suspicious Activity Reporting section of *The Regulatory Reporting Handbook*.)

Federal law provides a safe harbor from prosecution under the Right to Financial Privacy Act for all BSA required reports (see related section in this *Handbook*). Regulators currently believe that this safe harbor applies to information reported on the SAR and CTRs filed for currency transactions equaling or exceeding $10,000.

VI. Structuring

The BSA and related regulations prohibit "structuring" of transactions for the purpose of evading reporting and recordkeeping requirements. Structuring of a transaction occurs when a person conducts or attempts to conduct one or more currency transactions in any manner, for the purpose of evading BSA reporting requirements.

Financial institution employees must avoid any appearance of assisting customers in avoiding CTR filing and Monetary Instrument recordkeeping requirements. A bank employee may explain the law but may not, in response to a customer's questions, suggest that a proposed currency deposit be broken down so that a CTR will not be required or an entry in the Monetary Instrument recordkeeping system will not be required. Any employee who takes part in such activity may have "assisted in structuring."

Furthermore, employees may not act with willful blindness and deliberately avoid positive knowledge of structuring. If an employee has reason to suspect that someone is conducting transactions in a manner designed to avoid reporting or recording required by law, but the employee deliberately omits making further inquiries because he/she wishes to remain ignorant, the employee (and the institution) is deemed to have knowledge. Employees who have assisted in structuring expose themselves and their employers to potential civil and criminal penalties.

VII. Funds Transfers

Effective May 28, 1996, financial institutions located within the United States that initiate, transmit, or receive funds transfers must obtain, keep, and transmit specified information about the sender and recipient of the funds.

The rule applies to a broad range of methods for moving funds, including:

- Certain internal transfers, e.g., when a bank transfers funds from an originator's account to a beneficiary's account at the same bank (if the originator and beneficiary are different parties); and

- Payment orders made in person or by telephone, facsimile, or electronic messages sent or delivered by a customer or by a nonbank financial institution ("NBFI") on behalf of a customer to the NBFI's bank.

The Parties Involved

The rule was recently amended to conform definitions to those in the Uniform Commercial Code. Following is a brief description of the parties involved.

Originator

The originator is the sender of the first payment order. In the case of a funds transfer on behalf of a trust or a corporation, the corporation or the trust, and not the trustee or individual(s) authorized to issue the payment order on behalf of the trust or corporation, is the originator. Under the original rule, a foreign institution accepting a payment order from a foreign customer was considered the originator. However, under the amended rule, the foreign customer is the originator, and the foreign institution is the originator's institution.

Beneficiary

The beneficiary is the party to be paid by the beneficiary's institution.

Originator's Institution

The originator's or originating institution is the institution receiving a payment order from the sender of the first payment order (the originator). A foreign bank accepting a payment order from a customer is considered the originator's institution, not the originator as under the old rule. Under the amended rule, the first U.S. institution that handles an incoming international funds transfer is an intermediary institution rather than the originator's institution as under the old rule.

Intermediary Institution

The intermediary institution is any institution receiving a funds transfer other than the originator's institution or the beneficiary's institution. This includes a correspondent institution.

Beneficiary's Institution

The beneficiary's institution is the institution identified in the payment order that is to credit the beneficiary's account or pay the beneficiary.

Recordkeeping Requirements

The recordkeeping rule applies to most funds transfers of $3,000 or more (or the foreign equivalent) that are completed by domestic financial institutions (including foreign institutions in the United States). The amount and type of information institutions will be required to retain depends upon the type of financial institution, its role in the transfer (originator's or beneficiary's institution or intermediary institution), and the relationship of the parties to the transaction to the institution (i.e., established/first-time customer, etc.).

Originator's Institution

For each payment order that it accepts, the originator's financial institution must collect and retain either the original, a copy, or an electronic record of information relating to the order, including:

- Name and address of the person placing the order;

- Amount of the payment order;

- Execution date of the payment order;

- Payment instructions received with the order;

- Identity of the beneficiary's bank;

- As many of the following items as are received with the payment order:

  — Name and address of the beneficiary;

  — Account number of the beneficiary; and

  — Any other specific identifier of the beneficiary.

If the institution has knowledge that the person placing the order is not the originator, the institution must collect and retain identifying information (i.e., social security, employer identification, alien registration, or passport number) about the originator (if that information is known by the person placing the order).

For nonestablished customers, in addition to retaining the above information, an institution must:

- Verify the identity of the person placing the order prior to accepting the order, if the order is made in person; and

- If the institution accepts the order, obtain and retain a record of the type of identification reviewed, the number of the document, as well as the taxpayer identification number (e.g., social security or employer identification number) or, if none, alien identification number or passport number and country of issuance.

If the institution accepts a payment order that was not made in person, it must obtain and retain the information specified above, along with a copy or record of the method of payment for the funds transfer.

Payment Order Information (The Travel Rule)

Originator's Institution

Effective May 28, 1996, the originator's institution must include in any outgoing payment order on any funds transfer system (except Fedwire) essentially the same information concerning the originator, the beneficiary, and the transaction. The institution must also include the originator's account number, if payment is ordered from an account. Although a foreign financial institution may be considered an originator's institution, only financial institutions located within the United States are subject to the requirements of the travel rule.

Until an institution completes its conversion to the expanded Fedwire format, orders sent via Fedwire must include only limited information. However, Treasury and the other regulatory agencies encourage institutions to include complete originator and beneficiary information in the optional fields of Fedwire orders. The CHIPS and S.W.I.F.T. systems currently accommodate the information required by the travel rule.

The travel rule is designed to assist in investigations of money laundering by making identifying information about originators and beneficiaries of wire transfers easily accessible.

Intermediary Institutions

For each order that it accepts, an intermediary must retain either the original, a copy, or an electronic record of the order. This record must include the information received from the originator's institution about the originator and the beneficiary.

When transmitting the order to the next institution, an intermediary institution must include the originator and beneficiary information received from the originator's institution, as well as the name of the originator's institution.

Beneficiary's Institution

For each order that it accepts, the beneficiary's institution must retain either the original, a copy, or an electronic record of the order. The retained information must include the data forwarded by the originator's institution about the originator and the beneficiary.

For nonestablished customers, in addition to retaining a record of the order, if the proceeds are delivered to the beneficiary or an agent in person, the institution must:

- Verify the recipient's identity;

- Retain information about the identification reviewed along with additional identifying information about the beneficiary.

If the proceeds are not delivered in person, the beneficiary's institution must:

- Retain a copy of the instrument used to effect payment; or

- Retain the information contained on the instrument and record the address of the person to whom it was sent.

Information Retrieval

Both the originator's and beneficiary's institutions, but not an intermediary, must have the ability to retrieve records by referring to the name, or, in some cases, the account number, of the originator/beneficiary. The institution need not retain this information in any particular manner. It is only required to have the ability to retrieve the information if properly requested to do so.

Exceptions to the Funds Transfer Rules

The rules do not cover funds transfers:

- Governed by the Electronic Fund Transfer Act of 1978; or

- Made through an automated clearinghouse, an ATM, or a point-of-sale system.

Additionally, certain transactions are not subject to the rules because the Treasury has deemed them to be less likely to involve money laundering. Transfers of funds where the originator and beneficiary are any of the following are not subject to the rule:

- A domestic bank or its wholly owned domestic subsidiary;

- A domestic broker or dealer in securities or its wholly owned domestic subsidiary; or

- A federal, state, or local government, agency, or instrumentality.

Funds transfers where both the originator and beneficiary are the same person and the originator's and beneficiary's institution is the same domestic bank or same domestic broker or dealer in securities are also excluded from the rule.

VIII. Know Your Customer Requirements

Treasury Department officials have continued to indicate that they will issue regulations requiring financial institutions to adopt "Know Your Customer" policies and procedures. When issued, these rules will apply to both bank and nonbank financial institutions. In the absence of regulations, there are indications that regulators expect institutions to have some form of these policies and procedures already in place.

Institutions should have a clear and concise understanding of customers' practices. According to regulatory examination guidance, an effective "Know Your Customer" policy must, at a minimum, contain a clear statement of management's expectations and establish specific line responsibilities. Institutions should:

- Make a reasonable effort to determine the true identity of all customers requesting the institution's services;

- Take special care to identify the ownership of all accounts and of those using safe-custody facilities;

- Obtain identification from all new customers;

- Obtain identification from customers seeking to conduct significant business transactions; and

- Be aware of any unusual transaction activity or activity that is disproportionate to the customer's known business.

Know Your Customer

Know Your Customer policies should address both individual and business accounts. The same procedures that are prudent for business purposes in analyzing a prospective loan customer are also appropriate for BSA Know Your Customer purposes. The procedures should include obtaining the articles of incorporation and conducting a credit check of a proposed corporate deposit customer.

Regulators indicate that there is an inherent conflict in properly "knowing your customer" when a relationship manager is responsible for doing the background check of the customer and, at the same time, has a commission-based compensation. In such a situation, the institution should:

- Have a credit committee sign off as having reviewed the background check information; and

- Conduct regular audits of the customer background checks.

Where a relationship manager or account officer joins a new institution and brings along customers from his/her former employer, Know Your Customer information must be adequately completed at the new institution. The information is especially important for private banking services. It is insufficient for the background information to state that the customer was a client with the officer's employer for several years. The officer should adequately document the customer's source of funds and bank relationships.

The documentation regarding a client's source of funds must be fairly comprehensive. It is inadequate, for example, for the background information to report the source as "interest from inheritance." Documentation should state from whom the inheritance was received.

IX. Forfeiture

The U.S. Criminal Code provides for civil and criminal forfeiture of property, including collateral securing loans, that is derived from criminal activity. Criminal activity includes violation of the money laundering statutes. Under the forfeiture law, the government's interest in the property takes effect at the time of the illegal act. When a creditor is the subject of a forfeiture action, financial institutions risk both loss of collateral and diminution of the creditor's overall liability to meet credit obligations.

Federal law provides an innocent owner exception to protect the interest of an owner who proves that it had no "knowledge or consent" regarding the offense giving rise to the forfeiture. Generally, an institution can avoid loss of its collateral if it proves that it had no knowledge or consent regarding the criminal offense giving rise to the collateral. Moreover, employees may not act with willful blindness to deliberately avoid positive knowledge of the customer's criminal activity.

In a recent case unrelated to money laundering or the BSA, the U.S. Supreme Court ruled against an innocent owner where state law permitted seizure of property. The decision is based on state law and does not specifically affect seizures under federal laws, such as the BSA. However, financial institutions should be aware that the Court could easily extend the ruling to BSA-related seizures if presented with a case on the subject.

Financial institutions should review existing policies and procedures to assure adequate loan scrutiny, documentation, and monitoring. In addition to relying on credit quality, institutions must emphasize "Know Your Customer" procedures to avoid collateral loss or diminution of creditworthiness due to a forfeiture.

X. Transportation of Currency and Monetary Instruments ("CMIR")

Each person who, at any one time, physically transports or causes to be transported to any place outside the United States over $10,000 in currency or monetary instruments, or each person who receives the same from anywhere outside the United States, is required to file a Report of International Transportation of Currency or Monetary Instruments, Form 4790 (CMIR) with the U.S. Customs Service.

"Person" includes both individuals and firms. "Monetary instrument" includes all checks, drafts, notes, money orders, and other similar instruments that are drawn on or by a foreign financial institution and are not in bearer form, in addition to currency, bearer form negotiable instruments, and securities in bearer form. Treasury is currently revising the CMIR and accompanying regulations. Although "foreign financial institution" has not yet been defined, the definition will likely exclude U.S. branches and agencies of foreign banks. "At one time" is generally defined as on one calendar day or on one or more days if the person is attempting to evade the reporting requirement.

Funds transfers are not reported on CMIR forms because they do not involve the "physical" transportation of currency.

CMIR Filing

CMIR filing is solely the duty of the individual or firm who transports or receives currency or other monetary instruments in an aggregate amount exceeding $10,000. Financial institutions are not responsible for filing a CMIR on behalf of their customers when the customer imports or exports currency or monetary instruments in excess of $10,000, or when the customer asks the institution to carry out a transaction for the customer.

If a person physically transports monetary instruments into or out of the country, a CMIR must be filed at the time of entry into or departure from the United States. When a person receives currency or monetary instruments shipped from any place outside of the United States, a CMIR must be filed with the U.S. Customs Service within 15 days of receiving the currency or monetary instruments.

Common Carrier Exemption

An institution is exempt from filing the CMIR when it ships currency or monetary instruments that exceed $10,000 through the postal service or by common carrier. If the institution uses its own employees or a private courier service (other than an armored car service) it must file a CMIR.

Financial Institution Responsibilities

If a financial institution has knowledge that the currency for a deposit has come from abroad, the institution should inform the customer of the CMIR reporting requirement. If the institution knows that the customer is disregarding the reporting requirement or if the information about the transaction is suspicious, the institution should not file a CMIR, but should file a Suspicious Activity Report and also contact the local U.S. Customs office or call 1-800-BE ALERT.

XI. Foreign Bank Account Reporting (FBAR)

Financial institutions must annually file the Report of Foreign Bank and Financial Accounts, Form TDF 90-22.1 (commonly referred to as "FBAR") with the IRS Data Center in Detroit, Michigan, on or before June 30, for the prior calendar year if they have a financial interest in or signature or other authority over one or more foreign bank accounts, securities accounts, or financial accounts that, when aggregated, exceed $10,000 in value at any time during the calendar year.

An institution has a financial interest in such an account if it is the owner of record, has legal title, or is acting as fiduciary.

XII. Compliance Program

Federal law requires that all financial institutions establish and maintain a program to assure and monitor compliance with the requirements of the BSA and the Treasury regulations implementing the act.

The program developed by an institution must:

- Provide for the continued administration of the institution's policies and procedures;
- Be reasonably designed to assure and monitor compliance with the recordkeeping and reporting requirements;
- Be reduced to writing; and
- Be approved by the board of directors and reflected in the minutes of the financial institution.

Program Elements

The BSA compliance program must, at a minimum:

1. *Provide for a system of internal controls.* At a minimum such a system should:

- Identify reportable transactions at a point where all of the information necessary to properly complete the required reporting forms can be obtained.

- Ensure that all required reports are completed accurately and properly filed.

- Ensure that customer exemptions are properly granted and recorded.

- Provide for adequate supervision of employees who accept currency transactions, complete reports, grant exemptions, or engage in any other activity covered by the BSA.

- Establish dual controls and provide for separation of duties.

2. *Provide for independent testing of compliance.* Compliance testing should include, at a minimum:

- A test of the institution's internal procedures for monitoring compliance with the BSA, including interviews of employees who handle cash transactions and their supervisors.

- A sampling of large currency transactions followed by a review of CTR filings.

- A test of the validity and reasonableness of the customer exemptions granted by the institution.

- A test of the institution's recordkeeping system for compliance with the BSA.

- Documentation of the scope of the testing procedures performed and the findings of the testing. Any apparent violations, exceptions, or other problems noted during the testing procedures should be reported promptly to the board of directors or appropriate committee thereof.

3. *Designate an individual(s) to be responsible for coordinating and monitoring compliance with the Bank Secrecy Act.* To meet the minimum requirement, each institution must designate a senior official to be responsible for overall BSA compliance. In addition, other individuals in each office, department, or regional headquarters may be given the responsibility for day-to-day compliance.

4. *Train appropriate personnel.* At a minimum, the institution's training program must provide training of tellers and other personnel who handle

currency transactions. In addition, an overview of the BSA requirements should be given to new employees, and efforts should be made to keep executives informed of changes and new developments in BSA regulation.

XIII. Other Recordkeeping Requirements

> Institutions must retain, for five years, all records required under the Bank Secrecy Act. Institutions should have written policies and procedures confirming their adherence to this requirement.

Institutions must retain for five years all records required by the BSA laws and regulations. These records should be accessible within a reasonable period of time.

Institutions must also retain the following records as original, microfilm, or other copy or reproduction (front and back) for five years:

1. A record of each extension of credit that exceeds $10,000, which contains the name and address of the borrower, the amount, the nature or purpose of the borrowing, and the date of the loan. Loans secured by an interest in real property are exempted.

2. A record of each advice, request, or instruction received from or given to another financial institution or other person wherever located, regarding any transaction resulting (or intended to result and later canceled if such a record is normally made) in the transfer of currency or other monetary instruments, funds, checks, investment securities, or credit, of more than $10,000 to or from any person, account, or place outside the United States.

3. Each item, including checks, drafts, or transfers of credit, of more than $10,000 remitted or transferred to a person, account, or place outside the United States.

4. A social security number or taxpayer identification number (TIN) for each deposit account opened after June 30, 1972, and for each certificate of deposit sold or redeemed after May 31, 1978. The institution has 30 days to obtain the number, but will not be held in violation of the regulations if it maintains a list of the names, addresses, and account numbers of those customers from whom it has been unable to secure an identification number. For individuals who are nonresident aliens, the institution must record the person's passport number or a description of some other government document used to verify his identity.

A TIN is not required for accounts or transactions with the following: (i) agencies and instrumentalities of federal, state, local, or foreign governments; (ii) judges, public officials, or clerks of courts of record as custodians of funds in controversy or under the control of the court; (iii) aliens who are (a) ambassadors, ministers, career diplomatic, or consular officers, or (b) naval, military, or other attaches of foreign embassies and legations, and for the members of their immediate families; (iv) aliens who are accredited representatives of international organizations entitled to enjoy privileges, exemptions, and immunities as an international organization under the International Organization Immunities Act of December 29, 1945 (22 U.S.C. 288), and the members of their immediate families; (v) aliens temporarily residing in the United States for a period not to exceed 180 days; (vi) aliens not engaged in a trade or business in the United States who are attending a recognized college or university or any training program, supervised or conducted by any agency of the federal government; (vii) unincorporated subordinate units of a tax-exempt central organization that are covered by a group exemption letter; and (viii) nonresident aliens who are not engaged in a trade or business in the U.S.

5. Each document granting signature authority over each deposit or share account, including any notations, if such are normally made, of specific identifying information verifying the identity of the signer (such as a driver's license number or credit card number).

6. Each statement, ledger card, or other record on each deposit or share account, showing each transaction in, or with respect to, that account.

7. Each check, clean draft, or money order drawn on the institution or issued and payable by it, except those drawn for $100 or less or those drawn on accounts that can be expected to have drawn on them an average of at least 100 checks per month over the calendar year or on each occasion on which such checks are issued, and which are (i) dividend checks, (ii) payroll checks, (iii) employee benefit checks, (iv) insurance claim checks, (v) medical benefit checks, (vi) checks drawn on government agency accounts, (vii) checks drawn by brokers or dealers in securities, (viii) checks drawn on fiduciary accounts, (ix) checks drawn on other financial institutions, or (x) pension or annuity checks; each item in excess of $100 (other than charges or periodic charges made pursuant to agreement with the customer), comprising a debit to a customer's deposit or share account, not required to be kept, and not specifically exempted.

8. A record of each remittance or transfer of funds, or of currency, other monetary instruments, checks, investment securities, or credit, of more than $10,000 to a person, account, or place outside the United States.

9. Each check or draft in an amount in excess of $10,000 drawn on or issued by a foreign bank that the domestic bank has paid or presented to a nonbank drawee for payment.

10. Each item, including checks, drafts, or transfers of credit, of more than

$10,000 received directly and not through a domestic financial institution, by letter, cable, or any other means, from a bank, broker, or dealer in foreign exchange outside the United States.

11. A record of each receipt of currency, other monetary instruments, investment securities, or checks, and of each transfer of funds or credit, of more than $10,000 received on any one occasion directly and not through a domestic financial institution, from a bank, broker, or dealer in foreign exchange outside the United States.

12. For demand deposits only, records prepared or received by an institution in the ordinary course of business, which would be needed to reconstruct a transaction account and to trace a check in excess of $100 deposited in such account through its domestic processing system or to supply a description of a deposited check in excess of $100.

13. A record containing the name, address, and taxpayer identification number, if available, of the purchaser of each certificate of deposit, as well as a description of the instrument, a notation of the method of payment, and the date of the transaction.

14. A record containing the name, address, and taxpayer identification number, if available, of any person presenting a certificate of deposit for payment, as well as a description of the instrument and the date of the transaction.

15. Each deposit slip or credit ticket reflecting a transaction in excess of $100 or the equivalent record for direct deposit or other wire transfer deposit transactions. The slip or ticket shall record the amount of any currency involved.

XIV. Registration of Nondepository Institutions

As required by the Money Laundering Suppression Act of 1994, nondepository institutions offering the following services must register with the Treasury Department:

- Check cashing;

- Currency exchange;

- Money transmitting or remittance; or

- Selling or paying money orders or travelers' checks and other similar instruments.

These businesses must register with Treasury whether or not they are licensed by a state.

References

Laws:

    18 U.S.C. 981 et seq.
    18 U.S.C. 1956 et seq.
    31 U.S.C. 5311 et seq.

Regulations:

    12 CFR 21.21 (OCC)
    12 CFR 208.14 (FRB)
    12 CFR 326.8 (FDIC)
    12 CFR 563.177 (OTS)
    31 CFR 103 (Treasury Department)

Agency Guidelines:

    FDIC: FIL 30-95 (Payable Through Accounts)
    FRB: SR 95-10 (SUB) (Payable Through Accounts)
    Federal Reserve Bank Secrecy Act Manual

IV. Community Reinvestment Act

Introduction and Purpose 46

Assessment Area 46

Statement 47

Public Files 48

Performance Evaluations 49

Lending, Investment, and Service Tests 50

Community Development Test 52

Small Institution Performance Standards 53

Strategic Plan 53

Branch Closings 54

Data Collection, Reporting, and Disclosure 55

References 56

Introduction and Purpose

The Community Reinvestment Act (CRA) (12 U.S.C. 2901 et seq.), originally enacted in 1977, is intended to encourage financial institutions to help meet the credit needs of their entire communities, including low- and moderate-income neighborhoods. The Act neither prohibits any activity nor attempts to allocate credit or encourage unsound lending practices.

The financial regulatory agencies conduct evaluations of all insured depository institutions in order to assess their performance in meeting the credit needs of their local communities. The agencies must take these CRA assessments into account when ruling on a financial institution's applications.

An institution's obligations under the CRA rule can be divided into four primary categories:

- CRA statement;
- Public file maintenance;
- Performance; and
- Data collection, reporting, and disclosure.

Assessment Area

The federal regulatory agencies will evaluate an institution's CRA performance within one or more assessment areas that an institution defines. For all institutions except wholesale/limited purpose institutions, the assessment area(s) must include:

- One or more Metropolitan Statistical Areas (MSA) or counties, cities, or towns; and
- The areas where the institution has its main office, branches, and deposit-taking ATMs along with the surrounding census tracts where the institution has originated or purchased a substantial portion of its loans.

For wholesale or limited purpose institutions, the assessment area(s) must consist of one or more MSAs or counties, cities, or towns where the institution has its main office, branches, and deposit-taking ATMs.

If an institution's service area extends substantially beyond a state boundary, the institution must delineate separate assessment areas for the areas within each state.

Statement

Under the current rule, each institution's board of directors is required to adopt and review annually a CRA statement documenting its CRA programs. The CRA statement must include:

1. A map (or maps) delineating the area(s) surrounding each branch or office site.

Exercise particular care to assure that no lower- or middle-income areas that could reasonably be included in the delineation are excluded in the creation of these boundaries.

Standardized maps, such as those of Metropolitan Statistical Areas, may be useful in defining these boundaries. Another method of determining community service boundaries is to define the prime lending area of an institution, that is, the area within which most of its lending is done, and all other areas equally distant from the office.

Institutions with many branches may consider an entire metropolitan area to make up its community base. Institutions with widely dispersed branches may have a number of community areas to designate. Each office of an institution may have its own community area with some boundaries overlapping those of other offices. Institutions in rural areas may consider community areas to be as large as counties.

2. A list of the credit programs the institution is willing to offer in the community.

While a list unique to each local community served by the institution is not required by CRA, an institution should prepare separate lists if the communities clearly have disparate needs. One listing is appropriate for institutions serving more than one community with generally similar credit needs.

3. A copy of the institution's publicly posted CRA notice.

The CRA notice is a sign that must be displayed in all branches and offices of the institution. The CRA notice must state the following:

- The institution's CRA statement is available upon request (current rule only).

- Written comments relating to the institution's performance in the community may be submitted to the institution or its supervisory agency.

- All written comments relating to the institution's performance in the community are available to the public.

48 Consumer Banking Regulatory Handbook

- The institution's CRA Performance Evaluation is available to the public.

- The public may request announcements of the institution's application that would be affected by substandard CRA compliance.

In addition to the information above, the public notice must specify that the following information is available to the public:

- A map showing the assessment area where the branch is located;

- Information about the branches in the assessment area;

- A list of services provided at the branches in the area; and

- Data on lending performance in the assessment area.

Although not required in a CRA statement, an institution also should maintain a description of: how its programs are effectively meeting community credit needs; the ongoing work of the institution to remain informed about what those needs are; and its communication with members of the community regarding special credit services and opportunities available to the local community.

Public Files

Each institution must maintain a file, readily available for public inspection at the home office, and at least one designated office within each community area it serves, that includes:

- Copies of all CRA statements issued within the last two years (current rule only);

- A copy of the institution's most recent CRA Performance

- Evaluation (this must be placed in the file within 30 days of receipt); and

- Copies of all written comments received within the last two years regarding the institution's CRA Performance Evaluation or other references to its efforts to meet community credit needs.

In addition to the information specified above, the public file must contain:

- A list of the institution's branches, their street addresses, and census tracts;

- A list of services (including hours of operation, available loan and deposit products, and transaction fees) generally offered at the institution's branches and descriptions of material differences in the availability or cost of services at particular branches, if any. An institution may choose to include information regarding the availability of alternative systems for delivering retail banking services; and

- A map of each assessment area showing the boundaries of the area and identifying the census tracts contained within the area, either on the map or in a separate list.

The following institutions must keep additional information in the public file.

- *Institutions other than small banks* must include the CRA Disclosure Statement (provided to the institution by its regulator) for each of the two prior calendar years. If the institution elects to have consumer loans considered under the lending test, the institution must include the number and amount of the loans along with specified data covering each of the two prior years.

- *Institutions required to report HMDA data* must include a copy of the HMDA Disclosure Statement pertaining to the institution for each of the two prior calendar years. An institution that elects to have the regulatory agencies consider the mortgage lending of an affiliate for any of these years must include the affiliate's HMDA Disclosure Statement.

- *Small institutions* must include the loan-to-deposit ratio for each quarter of the prior calendar year.

- *Institutions with approved strategic plans* must include a copy of the plan.

Regulators also encourage institutions to include a written response to their CRA performance reports in the public file.

Each branch must maintain a copy of the public section of the institution's most recent CRA Performance Evaluation and a list of services provided by the branch, along with all the information in the public file relating to the assessment area where the branch is located.

Performance Evaluations

The financial regulatory agencies assess the record of each institution's performance in helping to meet the credit needs of its entire community. The regulators issue a rating and an evaluation report available for public disclosure. The four rating categories are: Outstanding, Satisfactory, Needs to Improve, and Substantial Noncompliance.

In the rating and evaluation report, under the current rule, the regulators will review the institution's CRA statement and any signed, written comments by the institution or the regulator, and will consider the following 4 assessment factors in evaluating the institution's record of performance.

- Lending, investment, and services tests (for large retail institutions);

- Community development test (for wholesale and limited purpose institutions);

- Small institution performance standards; and

- Strategic plan.

Lending, Investment, and Service Tests

Beginning July 1, 1997, the federal regulatory agencies will evaluate large retail institutions (those that have more than $250 million in assets or that are part of a holding company that has more than $1 billion in assets) on the basis of lending, investment, and service tests.

Lending Test

The lending test evaluates an institution's record of helping meet credit needs through lending activities in its assessment area(s). Performance under the lending test is crucial in order for an institution to obtain an acceptable overall assigned CRA rating. An institution must obtain at least a "low satisfactory" on the lending test in order to receive an assigned rating of "satisfactory" or higher.

An institution's performance on the lending test also may make up for lower ratings under the investment and service tests. If an institution receives an "outstanding" rating on the lending test, the regulation requires that the institution receive an assigned rating of at least "satisfactory."

Scope of Test

Under the lending test, the federal regulatory agencies will consider home mortgage, small business, small farm, and community development lending. If consumer lending constitutes a substantial majority of an institution's business, the regulator will evaluate the institution's consumer lending in one or more of the categories of covered loans, including motor vehicle, credit card, home equity, other secured, and other unsecured loans. The regulatory agencies will consider both loan originations and purchases.

At the institution's option and with certain limitations, the regulatory agencies will consider loans made by an affiliate in assessing performance under the lending test.

Performance Criteria

The regulatory agencies will evaluate an institution's lending performance according to the following criteria:

- *Lending activity* (number and amount of covered loans in assessment area(s));

- *Geographic distribution of loans;*

- *Borrower characteristics;*

- *Community development lending* (includes number and amount of community development loans along with complexity and innovativeness); and

- *Innovative or flexible lending standards.*

Investment Test

Under the investment test the regulator will evaluate an institution's record of helping meet its community's credit needs through qualified investments that benefit the assessment. The regulators may review also investments in a broader statewide or regional area that includes the assessment area(s). Activities considered under the lending or service tests may not be considered under the investment test. The regulatory agencies will consider, at the institution's option, an investment made by an affiliate.

Performance Criteria

The regulatory agencies evaluate an institution's investment performance according to the amount, innovativeness, responsiveness to the credit and community development needs and the degree to which the investments are not provided by private investors.

Service Test

The service test evaluates an institution's record of helping to meet credit needs in the assessment area(s) by analyzing an institution's community development services and the availability and effectiveness of an institution's systems for delivering retail banking services. At the institution's option, the regulatory agencies will consider a community development service provided by an affiliate.

Performance Criteria

Under the service test, the regulatory agencies will evaluate both the retail banking and community development services an institution provides.

In evaluating retail banking services, the regulatory agencies will evaluate the availability and effectiveness of an institution's systems for delivering retail banking services according to the following criteria:

- Distribution of branches among income group census tracts;

- Record of opening and closing branches;

- Availability and effectiveness of alternative service delivery systems (ATMs, banking by telephone, loan production offices, etc.) in low- and moderate-income areas and to low- and moderate-income individuals; and

- Range of services provided in the income group census tracts and the degree to which the services are tailored to meet the needs of those areas.

In assessing an institution's community development services, the regulatory agencies consider the extent to which the institution provides community development services and the innovativeness and responsiveness of community development services.

Community Development Test
(Wholesale/Limited Purpose Institutions)

The federal regulatory agencies will use the community development test to assess a wholesale or limited purpose institution's CRA performance record. This test evaluates the community development lending, qualified investments, or community development services that an institution provides in its assessment area(s). In order for an institution to qualify for the test, an institution must file with its primary regulator a written request to be designated as a wholesale/limited purpose institution.

Performance Criteria

The regulatory agencies will evaluate the community development performance of a wholesale or limited purpose institution according to the:

- Number and amount of community development loans, qualified investments, or community development services;

- Use of innovative investments, community development loans, or community development services and the extent to which the investments are not routinely provided by private investors; and

- Institution's responsiveness to credit and community development needs.

Small Institution Performance Standards

Small institutions (those having less than $250 million in assets and not belonging to a holding company that has more than $1 billion in assets) qualify for a streamlined examination process. The regulatory agencies use the streamlined assessment process for an institution that met these criteria during the prior calendar year.

Alternatively, a small institution may choose to be evaluated under the lending, investment, and services tests; the community development test; or under an approved strategic plan.

Performance Criteria

The regulatory agencies evaluate a small institution's record of helping to meet the community's credit needs under the following criteria:

- Loan-to-deposit ratio;

- Percentage of loans and other lending-related activities in the assessment area(s);

- Record of lending to and engaging in other lending-related activities for borrowers of different income levels and businesses and farms of different sizes;

- Geographic distribution of loans; and

- Record of taking action, if warranted, in response to written complaints about its performance in helping to meet credit needs in its assessment area(s).

Strategic Plan

As an alternative to the lending, investment, and services tests, any institution may choose to have its performance evaluated under a strategic plan if the:

- Institution submitted the plan to its primary regulator at least three months before the proposed effective date;

- Primary regulator approved the plan; and

- Plan is in effect and the institution has been operating under an approved plan for at least one year.

Development of Strategic Plan

Public input is essential throughout the course of developing a strategic plan. Once the institution has developed a plan, it must formally seek comment for at least 30 days, by publishing a notice in at least one newspaper of general circulation in each assessment area covered by the plan. During the comment period, copies of the plan must be available for public review at all offices in any assessment area covered by the plan.

An institution's strategic plan must:

- Contain measurable goals for each assessment area covered;

- Address the lending, investment, *and* service test performance categories; and

- Emphasize lending and lending-related activities, unless the institution is designated as a wholesale or limited purpose institution.

The plan may contain a provision permitting the institution to elect to be evaluated under any other appropriate assessment test if the institution fails substantially to meet its plan goals.

In evaluating the plan's measurable goals, the primary regulator considers the:

- Extent and breadth of lending or lending-related activities;

- Amount and innovativeness, complexity, and responsiveness of the qualified investments; and

- Availability and effectiveness of the institution's systems for delivering retail banking services and the extent and innovativeness of the institution's community development services.

Branch Closings

Though not technically part of the Community Reinvestment Act, the FDIC Improvement Act of 1991 requires a financial institution to have a policy on branch closing, and to notify its federal regulator 90 days before closing a branch office. This notice must include the reasons for the closure and other information required by the regulator. The institution also must notify customers by mail at least 90 days in advance, and must post a notice in the branch at least 30 days before closing.

The advance notice rules do not apply to the closing of an automated teller machine, nor to branches operated temporarily after purchase of a failed institution. In addition, branch relocations are exempt from the advance notice requirements when the relocation is within the same neighborhood, and it leaves customers served by the closed branch substantially unaffected by the move.

Data Collection, Reporting, and Disclosure

The revised CRA rule has significant data collection, reporting, and disclosure requirements.

Data Collection

Every institution, with the exception of small institutions, must collect and retain specified data on small business or small farm loans originated or purchased. Small institutions electing to be evaluated under the lending, investment, and service tests also fall within this requirement. Institutions have the option of collecting specified data for consumer loans.

An institution choosing to have loans by its affiliates considered under the lending or community development tests or under an approved strategic plan must collect the same data that the institution itself would have collected if it had originated or purchased the loans.

Institutions that qualify for evaluation under the small institution performance standards, but that choose to be evaluated under the lending, investment, and service tests must collect the same data that larger institutions are required to collect.

Reporting

Every institution, excluding small institutions, must annually report by March 1, for the previous calendar year, data for the following:

- *Small business and small farm loan.* For each census tract where an institution originated or purchased loans, the aggregate number and amount of loans along with other specified data.

- *Community development loans.* The aggregate number and amount of community development loans originated or purchased.

- *Home mortgage loans.* For an institution required to report HMDA data, the location of each home mortgage loan application, origination, or purchase outside the home or branch office MSAs.

- *Other activities.* If an institution elects to have affiliate, consortium, or third-party lending considered in its CRA evaluation, or if a small institution chooses to be evaluated under the lending, investment, and service tests, the institution must report the appropriate data.

- *Assessment area.* Every institution, excluding small institutions, must report a list for each assessment area showing the census tracts within the area.

References

Laws:

12 U.S.C. 2901 et seq.
12 U.S.C. 1831p

Regulations:

12 CFR Part 25 (OCC)
12 CFR Part 228 (FRB)
12 CFR Part 345 (FDIC)
12 CFR Part 563e (OTS)

V. Consumer Leasing Act

Introduction and Purpose 58

Leases Covered 58

Leases Not Covered 58

Timing of Disclosures 58

Manner of Disclosures 58

Content of Disclosures 59

Renegotiations and Extensions 62

Advertising of Lease 62

Record Retention 62

Relation to State Law 62

Penalties and Liabilities 63

References 63

Introduction and Purpose

The Consumer Leasing Act (15 USC 1667) requires accurate and meaningful disclosure of the terms and conditions of personal property leases by financial institutions to individuals. These disclosures and other regulations allow consumers to compare various lease terms or to compare lease terms with credit terms. They also place limits on the size of balloon payments and specify some requirements on leasing advertisements.

Leases Covered

The Consumer Leasing Act applies to leases:

- Longer than four months in duration;
- Valued at less than $25,000;
- For personal property to be used for personal, family, or household use; and
- Made to a natural person.

Leases Not Covered

The Consumer Leasing Act does not apply to leases:

- To government agencies, instrumentalities, or organizations;
- Of property to be used for commercial or agricultural purposes;
- Of personal property that is incidental to the lease of real property provided that the lessee has no liability for the value of the property at the end of the lease, except for abnormal wear and tear, and has no option to purchase the leased property;
- Of real property; or
- That meet the definition of credit sale.

Timing of Disclosures

Disclosures must be made before the lease is consummated.

Manner of Disclosures

Clear and conspicuous disclosures may be made either on the lease contract, or agreement, or on a separate statement clearly identifying the transaction.

Some disclosures need to be segregated from other required information and contain only directly related material. These include: amount due at lease signing, payment schedule, total amount of periodic payments, other charges, total of payments, payment calculation, early termination notice, notice of wear and use standard, end of lease term, statement referencing nonsegregated disclosures, and rent.

Any applicable state provisions should be made below or separate from the required federal disclosures.

Content of Disclosures

Disclosures must contain:

- *Identification of the property*. A dated, written statement clearly identifying the name of the lessor and lessee.

- *Description of the property*. A description of the property to be leased.

- *Amount due at lease signing*. The total amount of initial payment required of the lessee at consummation, or by delivery, if delivery occurs after consummation. Components of this amount include: refundable security deposits, advance monthly payments or periodic payments, and capitalized cost reductions. In motor-vehicle leases, the lessor must itemize how the amount due will be paid, by type and amount, including any net trade-in allowance, rebates, noncash credits, and cash payments.

- *Payment schedule and total amount of periodic payments*. The number, amount, and due dates, or periods of payments under the lease and the total amount of such payments.

- *Other charges*. The total amount of all other charges, such as disposition and maintenance charges, that are not already included in the periodic payments.

- *Total of payments*. The total amount of payments, which include: the sum of the amount due at lease signing (less any refundable amounts), the total amount of periodic payments (less any portion of the periodic payment paid at lease signing), and other charges.

- *Payment calculation*. In motor vehicle leasing, a mathematical progression of how the scheduled periodic payment is derived. This includes: gross capitalized cost, capitalized cost reduction, adjusted capitalized cost, residual value, depreciation and any amortized amounts, rent charge, total of base periodic payments, lease term, base periodic payment, itemization of other charges, and total periodic payments.

- *Insurance.* Identification of the types of insurance, if any, required in connection with the lease. If provided and paid for by the lessor, specify the types and amounts of coverage and the cost to the lessee. If not provided and paid for by the lessor, specify the types and amounts of coverage required of the lessee.

- *Warranties or guarantees.* Identification of any express warranty or guarantee provided by the manufacturer of the leased property and available to the lessee. A full description of the warranty or guarantee is not necessary if it is a standard warranty or guarantee.

- *Maintenance responsibilities.* Identification of the party responsible for maintenance of the leased property, a description of the scope of the maintenance responsibility, and a description of what will be considered ordinary wear and tear on the property, if the lessor sets such standards.

- *Security interest.* A description of any security interest the lessor will hold or retain in connection with the lease, and clear identification of the property to which the security interest applies.

- *Penalties and other charges for delinquency.* The reasonable amount or method of determining the amount of any penalty for delinquent, defaulted, or late payments.

- *Purchase option.* A statement whether the lessee has the option to purchase the leased property and, if at the end of the lease, at what price it may be purchased or, if prior to the end of the lease, at what time and the price or method of determining the price for purchase.

- *Statement referencing nonsegregated disclosures.* A statement that the lessee should refer to the lease documents for additional information on: early termination, purchase options and maintenance responsibilities, warranties, late and default charges, insurance, and any security interests, if applicable.

- *Early termination.* A statement of the conditions under which the lease may be terminated by either party prior to the end of the lease, and the reasonable amount or description of the method for determining the amount of any penalty or other charge for early termination.

- *Liability between residual and realized values.* A statement that the lessee shall be liable for the differential between the residual value of the property and its realized value at early termination or at the end of the lease term, if such liability exists. Residual value is a reasonable approximation of the anticipated value of the property at the end of the lease. Realized value is the price received by the lessor for the leased property at disposition to the highest offer for disposition or the fair market value of the leased property. Realized value does not include any deduction for disposition costs.

- *Right of appraisal.* When the lessee's liability at early termination or at the end of the lease is based on the realized value of the leased property, a statement that the lessee may obtain, at the lessee's expense, a professional appraisal of the leased property by an independent third party of the value that could be realized at the sale of the leased property. This appraisal will be binding.

- *Liability at end of lease term based on the residual value.* When the lessee is liable at the end of the lease term for the difference between the residual value of the leased property and its realized value:

    — *Rent and other charges.* Rent and other charges paid by the lessee and required by the lessor.

    — *Excess liability.* A statement that, to the extent that the estimated residual value of the leased property at the end of the lease term exceeds the realized value by more than three times the average monthly lease payment, there is a rebuttable presumption that the estimated residual value is unreasonable and not in good faith. The lessor must disclose that the amount of the collection of such excess liability can be made after successful court action in which the lessor pays the lessee's attorney's fees, unless the excess liability is due to unreasonable wear and tear or excessive use.

    — *Mutually agreeable final adjustment.* A statement that the requirements of the above section do not preclude the right of a willing lessee to make any mutually agreeable final adjustment regarding such excess liability, provided such agreement is reached after the end of the lease term.

- *Fees and taxes.* The dollar amount for all license fees, registration, title, or taxes required to be paid in connection with the lease.

If any of the above required disclosure information is not known at the time of disclosure, the lessor must provide an estimate of the unknown information and clearly identify it as an estimate.

Renegotiations and Extensions

New disclosures must be made whenever a lease is renegotiated or extended, except in the following cases:

- There is a reduction in the rent charge;

- One or more payments have been deferred, whether or not a fee was charged;

- The lease is extended for a period of six months or less;

- The leased property has been substituted with property that has substantially equivalent or greater economic value and no other lease terms have changed;

- In a multiple-item lease, when a new item is provided or a previously leased item is returned and the change in the average monthly payment is less than 25 percent; and

- If there is an agreement resulting from a court proceeding.

Advertising of Lease

Leasing opportunities must be described clearly as such in advertisements. Specific terms of the leasing must be included. Only terms that are or will be available in the future may be advertised. When "triggering" terms are used in advertisements, additional information must be given as well. Radio and television advertisements must refer either to a toll-free number or to a written advertisement in a publication where consumers may obtain this information. Any advertised table or schedule of lease terms must be clear and conspicuous. The lessee's liability must be clear and conspicuous in all advertisements.

Record Retention

A financial institution shall maintain disclosure information and compliance materials for at least two years.

Relation to State Law

A state law that is inconsistent with the requirements of the Consumer Leasing Act is preempted to the extent of the inconsistency. The Board may, however, grant an exemption from the requirements of the Act for any class of lease transactions within the state if the Board determines that:

Consumer Leasing Act 63

- The class of leasing transactions subject to state law requirements are substantially similar to the Act, or the lessees are given greater protection under state law; and

- There is an adequate provision for state enforcement.

Penalties and Liabilities

There are both criminal and civil liability provisions for failure to properly disclose or otherwise comply with the Consumer Leasing Act.

References

Laws:

15 U.S.C. 1667

Regulations:

12 CFR Part 213 (Reg. M) (FRB)
12 CFR 545.53 (OTS)

VI. Credit Practices Rules

Introduction and Purpose 66

Transactions Covered 66

Prohibited Contract Provisions 66

Permitted Contract Provisions 66

Definition of Earnings 67

Definition of Household Goods 67

Prohibited Practices 68

Definition of a Cosigner 68

Definition of What a Cosigner Is Not 69

References 69

Introduction and Purpose

The Federal Reserve Board and the OTS have adopted Credit Practices Rules under Section 18(f)(1) of the Federal Trade Commission Act in response to a similar rule adopted by the FTC for creditors other than banks and savings associations. The rule is contained in 12 CFR 227 for banks and 12 CFR 535 for savings associations. The Credit Practices Rules are designed to assure the fairness of consumer credit, late charge accounting, and cosigner practices of financial institutions.

Transactions Covered

Credit Practices Rules apply to all consumer loans, regardless of size, except loans to finance the purchase of real estate. (Mobile homes and houseboats are not considered to be real estate if they are considered personal property under state law.) A "consumer" is a person who seeks or acquires goods, services, or money for personal, family, or household purposes.

Prohibited Contract Provisions

Under the Credit Practices Rules, a loan contract may not contain any of the following:

1. A "confession of judgment" or "warrant of attorney" in which the borrower waives the right to notice and the opportunity to be heard in the event of a suit to enforce an obligation;

2. A waiver of exemption by which the consumer relinquishes the statutory right to protect home, possessions, or wages from seizure to satisfy a judgment. (Waivers given in respect to property that will serve as security for an obligation are not covered in this rule.);

3. An assignment of wages by which the institution would be given the right to receive the consumer's wages or earnings directly from the consumer's employer; or

4. A nonpossessory security interest in household goods unless such goods are purchased with credit extended by the financial institution.

Permitted Contract Provisions

The Credit Practices Rules permit the following contract provisions:

1. Confessions of judgment executed after default or the filing of a suit on the debt;

Credit Practices Rules 67

2. Powers of attorney contained in a mortgage or deed of trust for foreclosure purposes or given to expedite the repossession or transfer of collateral;

3. Confessions of judgment in Louisiana for the purpose of executory process;

4. Waivers of demand, presentment, protest, notice of dishonor, and notice of protest and dishonor;

5. An assignment of wages that, by its terms, is revocable at any time by the consumer;

6. A payroll deduction or preauthorized payment plan (whether revocable or not by the consumer), effective at the start of the loan, for the purposes of making each payment;

7. An assignment of wages that have been earned at the time of the assignment;

8. Garnishment (a legal procedure allowing property belonging to a debtor to be turned over to a creditor);

9. Security interest in household goods not purchased with credit extended by the financial institution if the goods are placed in the financial institution's possession; and

10. Security interests in real and personal property of the consumer other than household goods.

Definition of Earnings

"Earnings" are compensation paid or payable for personal services rendered or to be rendered by the consumer (whether denominated as wages, salary, commission, or bonus), including periodic payments received from a pension, retirement, or disability program.

Definition of Household Goods

"Household goods" are defined as the clothing, furniture, appliance, linens, china, crockery, kitchenware, and personal effects of the consumer and the consumer's dependents.

Not considered to be household goods are works of art, electronic equipment (except one television and one radio), antiques (over 100 years old and retaining their original character and form), jewelry (other than wedding rings), fixtures, automobiles, boats, snowmobiles, cameras and camera equipment, pianos, home workshops, and the like.

68   Consumer Banking Regulatory Handbook

Prohibited Practices

1. *Pyramiding of late charges.*

Pyramiding is an accounting method by which multiple late charges are applied to a single delinquent payment. For example, a lender applies a late charge to a late payment when the payment is received, making the late payment short or insufficient. Subsequent payments may be received on time, but since the previous payment is considered short, a late charge is again applied. This continues until the borrower pays the late charge separately or until the loan matures. This should not be confused with situations where a *payment* has been missed, never made up, and continues to accumulate late charges each month until the missed payment is made to bring the account up to date.

2. *Misrepresentation by the institution of the nature and extent of a cosigner's liability.*

The institution must provide a clear and conspicuous notice to the cosigner before he or she becomes obligated to any credit program. The notice must be similar to the following statement:

"You are being asked to guarantee this debt. Think carefully before you do. If the borrower doesn't pay the debt, you will have to. Be sure you can afford to pay the debt if you have to, and that you want to accept this responsibility. You may have to pay up to the full amount of the debt if the borrower does not pay. You also may have to pay late fees or collection costs, which increase this amount. The bank can collect this debt from you without first trying to collect from the borrower. The bank can use the same collection methods against you that can be used against the borrower, such as suing you, garnishing your wages, etc. If this debt is ever in default, that fact may become a part of your credit record. This notice is not the contract that makes you liable for the debt."

Definition of a Cosigner

A "cosigner" (whether or not so denominated in the loan contract) means:

1. Any person who assumes personal liability, in any capacity, for the obligation of another customer without receiving goods, services, or money in return for the obligation. This includes any person whose signature is requested to allow a consumer to obtain credit or to prevent collection of a consumer's obligation that is in default;

Credit Practices Rules

2. For open-end credit, a person who signs the debt instrument but does not have the contractual right to obtain credit under the account.

Definition of What a Cosigner Is Not

A cosigner is not:

1. A spouse whose signature is required on a credit obligation to perfect a security interest in accordance with state law;

2. A person who does not assume personal liabilities, but who rather only provides collateral for the obligation of another person; or

3. A person who has the contractual right to obtain credit under an open-end account, whether exercised or not.

References

Laws:

15 U.S.C. 57a(f)

Regulations:

12 CFR Part 227 (Reg AA) (FRB)
12 CFR Part 535 (OTS)

VII. Deposit Insurance

Introduction and Purpose 72

Insured Deposits 72

Insurance Limit 72

Categories of Ownership 73

Pass-Through Insurance 74

Deposits Held on Another's Behalf 76

Determining Legal Ownership 76

Official Signs 77

Advertisements 77

References 77

Introduction and Purpose

The Federal Deposit Insurance Corporation (FDIC) insures the deposits of most U.S. depository institutions. The FDIC is an independent agency of the U.S. government established by Congress in 1933 to insure bank deposits, help maintain a sound banking system, and protect the nation's money supply in case of financial institution failure. In 1989, the FDIC was given the additional duty of insuring deposits in savings associations. As a result, the FDIC insures deposits in banks, using the Bank Insurance Fund (BIF), and insures deposits in savings associations, using the Savings Association Insurance Fund (SAIF). Both BIF and SAIF are backed by the full faith and credit of the United States.

Insured Deposits

Federal deposit insurance protects deposits that are payable in the United States. Deposits that are only payable overseas, and not in the United States, are not insured. A depositor does not have to be a citizen or resident of the United States to receive insurance protection.

All types of deposits received by an insured depository institution in its usual course of business are insured. For example, savings deposits, checking deposits, NOW accounts, Christmas Club accounts, and time deposits (including certificates of deposit) are all insured deposits. Cashier's checks, money orders, officer's checks, and outstanding drafts also are insured. Certified checks, letters of credit, and traveler's checks, for which an insured depository institution is primarily liable, are also insured when issued in exchange for money or its equivalent, or for a charge against a deposit account.

Insurance Limit

As limited by the categories of ownership rules, the FDIC insures each account up to $100,000. Accrued interest is included when calculating insurance coverage. Deposits in different depository institutions are insured separately, even if the institutions are owned by the same holding company.

Deposits maintained in different categories of legal ownership are separately insured. Accordingly, a depositor can have more than $100,000 insurance coverage in a single institution if such funds are owned and deposited- in different ownership categories. Federal deposit insurance is not determined on a per-account basis. A depositor cannot increase FDIC insurance by dividing funds owned in the same ownership category among different accounts.

Deposit Insurance 73

The most common categories of ownership are single (or individual) ownership, joint ownership, and testamentary accounts. Separate insurance is also available for funds held for retirement purposes, e.g., Individual Retirement Accounts, Keoghs, and pension or profit-sharing plans. Each of these categories of ownership is discussed in the "Categories of Ownership" section below.

Categories of Ownership

The following categories of ownership are relevant to determining the total deposit insurance coverage afforded to a depositor. Each section below includes a description of the type of account and its deposit insurance coverage.

Single Ownership Accounts

All single ownership accounts established by, or for the benefit of, the same person are added together and the total is insured up to a maximum of $100,000. A single (or individual) ownership account is an account owned by one person. Single ownership accounts include accounts in the owner's name, accounts established for the benefit of the owner by agents, nominees, guardians, custodians, or conservators, and accounts established by a business that is a sole proprietorship.

Joint Accounts

Joint accounts are insured separately (to a maximum of $100,000) from single ownership accounts if each of the following conditions is met:

- All co-owners are natural persons. Legal entities such as corporations or partnerships are not eligible for joint account deposit insurance coverage.

- Each of the co-owners must have a right of withdrawal on the same basis as the other co-owners.

- Each of the co-owners must have personally signed a deposit account signature card. The execution of an account signature card is not required for certificates of deposit, deposit obligations evidenced by a negotiable instrument, or accounts maintained by an agent, nominee, guardian, custodian, or conservator, but the deposit must in fact be jointly owned.

A deposit account held in two or more names that does not qualify for joint account deposit insurance coverage is treated as being owned by each named owner, as an individual, corporation, partnership, or unincorporated association, as the case may be, according to each co-owner's actual ownership interest.

If an individual owns and deposits funds in his or her own name but then gives another person the right to withdraw funds from the account, the account will be insured as a joint ownership account. There are two exceptions to this rule. First, withdrawals by a person other than the owner are permitted under a Power of Attorney. Second, withdrawals by a person other than the owner are permitted if the deposit account records clearly indicate, to the satisfaction of the FDIC, that the funds are owned by one person and that the other signatory is authorized to withdraw funds only on behalf of the owner.

The FDIC has separate rules for determining deposit insurance coverage for multiple joint accounts.

Gifts to Minors

Funds deposited for the benefit of a minor under the Uniform Gifts to Minors Act are added to any other single ownership accounts of the minor and the total is insured up to a maximum of $100,000.

Retirement Accounts

Until December 19, 1993, IRA and Keogh funds were insured separately from each other and from any other funds of the depositor.

Since December 19, 1993, IRA and Keogh funds have been separately insured from any nonretirement funds the depositor may have at an institution. However, IRA and self-directed Keogh funds are now added together, and the combined total is insured up to $100,000. IRA and self-directed Keogh funds are also aggregated with certain other retirement funds: namely, those belonging to other self-directed retirement plans, and those belonging to so-called "Plan" accounts, if the deposits are eligible for pass-through insurance.

Time deposits made prior to December 19, 1993, do not become subject to the aggregation rules until the deposits mature, roll over, or are renewed.

Pass-Through Insurance

The general rule is that deposits belonging to pension plans and profit-sharing plans (including self-directed IRA and Keogh plans, and 457 Plans) receive pass-through insurance. "Pass-through insurance" means that each beneficiary's ascertainable interest in a deposit — as opposed to the deposit as a whole — is insured up to $100,000.

In order for a pension or profit-sharing plan to receive pass-through insurance, the institution's deposit account records must specifically disclose the fact that the depositor (for instance, the plan itself, or its trustee) holds the funds in a fiduciary capacity. In addition, the details of the fiduciary relationship between the plan and its participants, and the participants' beneficial interests in the account, must be ascertainable from the institution's deposit account records or from the records that the plan maintains in good faith and in the regular course of business.

The pass-through rule applies to any deposit made by a pension or profit-sharing plan in any institution if the deposit was made before December 19, 1992.

The pass-through rule also applies to any new deposit made by a plan on or after December 19, 1992, if the deposit is made in an institution that meets the FDIC's standards for "well-capitalized" institutions.

Finally, the pass-through rule applies to any new deposit made by a plan on or after December 19, 1992, if the deposit is made in an institution that meets the FDIC's standards for "adequately capitalized" institutions, but only if the institution also satisfies either one of the following conditions:

- The institution has received a waiver from the FDIC to take brokered deposits ("brokered deposits" are ones that a depositor makes through an intermediary that is engaged in the business of placing funds for others); or

- The institution notifies the plan in writing, at the time the plan makes the deposit, that such deposits are eligible for pass-through coverage.

In all other cases, any deposit that a plan makes on or after December 19, 1992, does not receive pass-through insurance, but rather is insured as a whole up to $100,000 in total.

Rollovers and renewed deposits are considered to be "new" deposits.

If a deposit has pass-through insurance when it is made into an account, that particular deposit does not lose its pass-through insurance until the deposit matures, even if the institution falls out of compliance with the standards for pass-through insurance in the meantime. But once the institution falls out of compliance, any subsequent deposits that are made into that same account (including ones that are rollovers and renewals of earlier deposits) would not have pass-through insurance.

Disclosures

Since July 1, 1995, institutions must provide certain *written* disclosures.

For existing accounts:

- Upon request from an account administrator, the institution must disclose within five days its current prompt corrective action (PCA) capital category, tier I and total risk-based capital ratios, and provide a statement whether, in the institution's judgment, the deposits would be eligible for pass-through insurance;

- When the institution believes that an account is no longer eligible for pass-through insurance, it must notify all affected depositors within 10 business days of its new PCA capital category and that new, rolled-over, or renewed deposits will not be eligible for pass-through insurance (existing time deposits continue to receive pass-through insurance until maturity).

For new accounts:

- At the time a depositor opens an employee benefit account, the institution must disclose its PCA capital category, and provide a description of the requirements for pass-through insurance coverage along with a statement whether, in the institution's judgment, the deposits are eligible for pass-through insurance.

Other Trust-Related Accounts

Insurance coverage of trust-related accounts is discussed in *The* **PricewaterhouseCoopers** *Trust Regulatory Handbook for Financial Institutions.*

Deposits Held on Another's Behalf

Funds held or deposited by a party other than the borrower have different insurance coverage depending on the legal status of the relationship between the parties. The FDIC's insurance coverage rules address a variety of such accounts including those maintained by agents, custodians, fiduciaries, mortgage servicers, insurance companies, executors, and businesses.

Determining Legal Ownership

The FDIC presumes that funds are owned as shown on the "deposit account records" of the insured depository institution. If the FDIC determines that the deposit account records of the institution are unambiguous, those records are binding on the depositor. The "deposit account records" of an insured deposi-

Deposit Insurance

tory institution are account ledgers, signature cards, certificates of deposit, passbooks, and certain computer records. However, account statements, deposit slips, items deposited, and canceled checks are not considered deposit account records for purposes of calculating deposit insurance.

Official Signs

FDIC regulations describe the official signs of the FDIC and prescribe their use by insured depository institutions. There are two different official insurance signs. The official bank sign measures 7 by 3 inches and includes the letters FDIC with the FDIC seal nested inside the letter "C." The official savings association sign measures 5-1/8 inches in diameter, and displays the (bald eagle) official seal of the United States. Insured banks may display either the official bank sign or the official savings association sign. Savings associations may only display the savings association sign.

Insured depository institutions must continuously display an official insurance sign at each station or window where it receives insured deposits. Automatic service facilities, such as automated teller machines (ATMs), cash dispensing machines, point-of-sale terminals, and other electronic facilities, need only display an official sign if they receive deposits.

Advertisements

Insured depository institutions must include the official advertising statement in all advertisements, except as provided below. The official advertising statement is as follows: "Member of the Federal Deposit Insurance Corporation." The short title "Member of FDIC" or "Member FDIC" or a reproduction of the official symbol may be substituted. The official advertising statement must be clearly legible.

The non-English equivalent of the official advertising statement may be used in any advertisement, provided that FDIC approves the translation.

References

Laws:

12 U.S.C. 1811 et seq.

Regulations:

12 CFR Part 330
12 CFR Part 328

VIII. Electronic Fund Transfer Act

Introduction and Purpose 80

Transactions Covered 80

Transactions Not Covered 80

Issuance of Access Devices 80

Initial Disclosures 81

Terminal Receipt Disclosures 82

Periodic Statement Disclosures 82

Preauthorized Transfer Disclosures 83

Error Resolution Procedures 84

Consumer Liability 86

Notification of Unauthorized Transfer 88

References 88

Introduction and Purpose

The Electronic Fund Transfer Act (EFTA), as implemented by Regulation E, establishes the rights, liabilities, and responsibilities of financial institutions and consumers in electronic fund transfer systems.

Transactions Covered

EFTA applies to any electronic fund transfer (EFT), defined as any transaction initiated through an electronic terminal, telephone, computer, or magnetic tape that instructs a financial institution to either credit or debit a consumer's asset account established primarily for personal, family, or household purchases.

As a general rule, EFTA also covers preauthorized transfers to or from an account in a financial institution with over $25 million in assets.

Transactions Not Covered

Transactions specifically excluded from the definition of EFT are:

1. Check verification and guarantee services that do not result in a direct debit or credit to a consumer's account;

2. Transfers of funds for a consumer through Fedwire or other system that is used primarily for transfers between businesses and financial institutions;

3. Any EFT made for the purchase or sale of securities or commodities regulated by the SEC or CFTC;

4. Intrainstitutional EFTs such as automatic transfers from savings to deposit accounts, debiting of service charges, and automatic loan payments where the bank is the creditor;

5. Certain incidental telephone-initiated transfers not under a prearranged plan contemplating periodic or recurring transfers;

6. Transactions for trust accounts; and

7. Preauthorized transfers to or from accounts held at small financial institutions (assets of $100 million or less).

Issuance of Access Devices

In general, an institution may issue an access device (e.g., card, identification code) to each holder on an account only if the access device is:

1. Requested (in writing or orally) or applied for; or

Electronic Fund Transfer Act

2. A renewal of, or in substitution for, an accepted access device.

An institution may issue an unsolicited access device if it cannot be validated without an oral or written request from the consumer with reasonable verification of identity. Validation and disposal instructions, along with all necessary disclosures, must be provided.

EFTA and the Truth in Lending Act both govern the issuance of access devices, as follows:

1. *Electronic Fund Transfer Act:*

    a) Issuance of debit cards and other access devices without credit features;

    b) Addition of EFT capabilities to credit cards; and

    c) Issuance of access devices whose only credit feature is a preexisting agreement to extend credit to cover overdrafts or maintain minimum balances.

2. *Truth in Lending Act*

    a) Issuance of credit cards (see Reg. Z);

    b) Addition of a credit feature to a debit card or access device; and

    c) Issuance of dual debit/credit cards except for access devices whose only credit feature is a preexisting agreement to extend credit to cover overdrafts or maintain minimum balances.

Initial Disclosures

The institution must provide the consumer with the following written disclosures at the time a consumer contracts for an EFT service or before the first EFT is made:

1. Summary of the consumer's liability;
2. Address and telephone number of the person or office to notify in the event of loss or unauthorized use;
3. The institution's business days;
4. Types of allowed EFTs, with applicable limitations;
5. Any charges for EFTs or the right to make EFTs;
6. Consumer's right to receive EFT documentation;

7. Consumer's right to stop payment on a pre-authorized EFT, and the procedure for initiating a stop payment order;

8. Institution's liability for failure to make or stop EFTs;

9. Circumstances in which institution will disclose information to third parties; and

10. Consumer's rights and procedures regarding error resolution.

The institution must mail or deliver a written notice to the consumer at least 21 days before the effective date of any change in terms or conditions if the change would result in any of the following:

1. Increased fees or charges;

2. Increased liability for the consumer;

3. Fewer types of available EFTs; or stricter limitations on the frequency or dollar amount of transfers.

At least once each calendar year the institution must mail or deliver an error resolution notice to the consumer, or the institution must include it in the periodic statement.

Terminal Receipt Disclosures

Electronic terminals must make a receipt available at the time of the transfer, and the receipt must include the following, as applicable:

1. Amount of the transfer (including allowable fees if itemized on the receipt and posted at the terminal);

2. Calendar date of the transfer;

3. Type of transfer and account;

4. A number or code identifying the consumer, account, or access device used. The number or code does not have to be unique, and it need not exceed four digits or characters;

5. Location, or location code, of the terminal; and

6. The name of any third party to or from whom funds are transferred.

Periodic Statement Disclosures

An institution generally must send a periodic statement monthly if an EFT has occurred, or quarterly if no EFT has occurred. The statement must include, as applicable:

1. Amount of the transfer, including any charge;
2. Date the transfer was posted to the account;
3. Type of transfer(s) and account(s);
4. The location as it appeared on the receipt for each transfer (except for deposits to the consumer's account) initiated at an electronic terminal;
5. Name of any third-party payee or payor;
6. The account number(s) for which the statement is issued;
7. The total amount of EFT-related fees and charges;
8. The beginning and ending account balances;
9. The address and phone number for consumer inquiries; and
10. If provided, the phone number that the consumer can use to determine if a preauthorized transfer was made.

Where a consumer's passbook may not be accessed by an EFT other than preauthorized transfers to the account, a financial institution need not send a periodic statement, provided that the institution update the consumer's passbook or provide the required information at the consumer's request.

Preauthorized Transfer Disclosures

When an account is scheduled to be credited by a preauthorized EFT from the same payor at least once every 60 days, the institution must provide some form of notice to the consumer so that the consumer can determine if the transfer occurred.

If the payor does not provide notice to the consumer that the transfer has been initiated, the institution must do one of the following to provide notice to the consumer:

1. *Positive Notice.* Provide oral or written notice that a preauthorized transfer occurred within two business days of the transfer;
2. *Negative Notice.* Provide oral or written notice that a preauthorized transfer did not occur within two business days after the scheduled transfer date; or
3. *Telephone Access.* Provide an easily accessible telephone line that the consumer may call to make such determination. The institution must provide a number that the consumer can access without incurring long-distance charges.

Preauthorized credits to the consumer's account must be made on the day the funds are received, although the funds need not be available on the date credited.

The consumer must provide authorization for preauthorized transfers.

A consumer may stop payment of a preauthorized transfer, orally or in writing, up to three business days before the scheduled date of the transfer. If a written confirmation is required, the customer must be notified at the time of the oral request that a written confirmation must be provided within 14 days or the stop-payment order will cease to be binding.

In the event a transfer is scheduled that varies in amount from the previous transfer, the institution or designated payee must notify the consumer in writing of the amount at least 10 days before the scheduled transfer date. The consumer may elect to receive notice only when the amount varies by more than a specified amount or range.

Error Resolution Procedures

Definition of an "Error"

1. An unauthorized or incorrect EFT to or from a consumer's account;
2. An omission of an EFT from the consumer's periodic statement;
3. A computational or bookkeeping error by the institution relating to the EFT;
4. The consumer's receipt of an incorrect amount of money from an EFT terminal;
5. An EFT not identified by the institution, as required; or
6. A consumer's request for any documentation required to be provided under the EFTA, or for additional information or clarification concerning an EFT.

Notice of an Error

A notice of error is an oral or written notice that is received by the institution not later than 60 days after the institution transmits a periodic statement or other documentation that first reflects the alleged error.

The notice must enable the institution to determine the consumer's name and account number and, to the extent possible, the type, date, and amount of the error.

An institution may require a written confirmation of an oral error notice within 10 business days if the institution advises the consumer when the consumer gives oral notice.

Investigating the Error

The institution must promptly investigate the alleged error and determine whether an error occurred within 10 business days of receiving a notice of error.

If the institution is unable to complete its investigation within 10 days, the institution may take up to 45 calendar days provided it:

1. Provisionally recredits the funds, including interest, to the consumer's account within 10 business days;
2. Advises the consumer within two business days of the provisional recrediting; and
3. Gives the consumer full use of the provisionally recredited funds during the investigation.

If the financial institution has a reasonable basis for believing that an unauthorized transaction may have occurred, it may withhold a maximum of $50 from the amount recredited.

The institution need not provisionally recredit if it requires but does not receive timely written confirmation of an oral notice, or if the error involves an account subject to the margin requirements or other aspects of Regulation T.

If a notice of an error involves an EFT that was not initiated within a state or involves a point-of-sale debit card transaction, these 10- and 45-day time periods become 20 and 90 days, respectively.

An institution must report the result of its investigation to the consumer within three business days after completing the investigation. Compliance with this provision was not mandatory until January 1, 1997.

Resolving the Error

If an error has occurred, the institution must correct the error within one business day after the determination is made, including the crediting of interest and fees, as applicable. The institution must provide an oral or written report of the correction to the consumer within the 10/45-day time limits.

If no error (or a different error) is identified, the institution must mail a written explanation of its findings within three days after concluding its investigation, but within the 10/45-day time limits. The explanation must include a notice of the consumer's rights to request the documents relied upon by the institution.

Upon debiting a provisionally recredited amount, the institution must provide oral or written notice to the consumer of the date and amount of the debit and of the fact that the institution will honor (without charge) checks, drafts, and preauthorized transfers, to the extent they would have been honored if the provisional credit had not been debited, for a period of five business days from the date of notice.

Where an EFT also involves the extension of credit under an overdraft protection or minimum balance maintenance agreement, the institution must comply with the error resolution procedures of Regulation E rather than Regulation Z.

Consumer Liability

A consumer may be held liable for unauthorized EFTs only if:

1. The access device is accepted;
2. The institution has provided a means to identify the consumer to whom the access device was issued; and
3. The institution has provided the following written disclosures:

    a) Summary of the consumer's liability for unauthorized EFTs;

    b) Phone number and address for reporting unauthorized EFTs; and

    c) The institution's business days.

If the consumer notifies the institution *within two business days* after learning of the loss or theft of an access device, the consumer may be held liable for unauthorized transfers only to the lesser of:

1. $50; or
2. The amount of money or value of property or services obtained from the unauthorized transfers before the institution was notified or before it otherwise had reason to suspect that an unauthorized transfer involving the consumer's account has been or may be made.

If the consumer notifies the institution *more than two business days* after learning of the loss or theft of an access device, the consumer is liable for not more than $500 (up to $50 for transfers occurring during the first two business days, plus the amount of subsequent transfers) provided that the institution establishes that it could have prevented the unauthorized transfers that occurred after the two business days had it been notified earlier.

If the consumer fails to notify the institution *within 60 days* of transmittal of the periodic statement of any unauthorized transfer that appears on the periodic statement, the consumer's liability shall not exceed:

1. The lesser of $50 or the amount of money or value of property or services obtained from unauthorized transfers that were reflected on the periodic statement or occurred during the 60 days after the statement's transmittal; and

2. The amount of unauthorized transfers after the close of the 60-day period and before the institution is notified of the unauthorized transfer provided the institution can establish that it could have prevented those unauthorized transfers had the consumer reported the transfers within the 60-day period.

As a result of these rules, a consumer could have unlimited liability for transfers occurring after the 60-day period, in addition to $500 for transfers during this period, if:

1. The loss or theft of the card goes unreported for more than two business days after discovery;

2. Unauthorized transfers related to the loss or theft go unreported for 60 days after appearing on a periodic statement, regardless of whether an access device was involved; and

3. There are additional unauthorized transfers after the 60-day period.

If the delay in reporting is due to extenuating circumstances, the time periods for notification shall be extended to a reasonable time.

Lesser liability limits apply if imposed by state law or established by an agreement with the consumer.

Liability provisions of the EFTA apply to unauthorized EFTs initiated by a combined access device-credit card, including an access device with overdraft privileges. They do not apply to the unauthorized use of a combined access device-credit card when no EFTs are involved.

An institution may not charge a consumer for unauthorized EFTs because the consumer was negligent with the access device. In addition, it is a violation of the EFTA for an institution to state on disclosures that a consumer's keeping his or her personal identification number on an ATM card will release the institution from liability in the event of an unauthorized transfer.

**Notification of
Unauthorized Transfer**

Notice to an institution regarding unauthorized use is considered given when:

1. The consumer takes whatever steps are reasonably necessary to provide the institution with the pertinent information, whether or not any particular employee, in fact, receives the information. The consumer may give notice in person, by telephone, or in writing.

2. The institution becomes aware of circumstances that indicate an unauthorized transfer has been or may be made.

References

Laws:

15 U.S.C. 1693 et seq.

Regulations:

12 CFR 205 (Reg. E) (FRB)

IX. Equal Credit Opportunity Act

Introduction and Purpose 91

Loans Covered 91

General Antidiscrimination Rule 91

Types of Lending Discrimination 92

Advertising 93

Applications and Information Gathering 93

Written Applications 95

Application Processing and Evaluation 95

Appraisals 97

Credit Extension 98

Notification 100

Furnishing Credit Information 101

Record Retention 102

Indirect Lending Disclosure 102

Government Monitoring Information 102

Business Credit Exceptions 103

Agency Referrals 103

Corrective Action 104

Penalties 104

References 104

Equal Credit Opportunity Act

Introduction and Purpose

The primary focus of the Equal Credit Opportunity Act (ECOA) is to prevent discrimination in the granting of credit. ECOA, as implemented by Regulation B, became effective in 1975 and makes it unlawful to discriminate on a prohibited basis with respect to any aspect of a credit transaction.

In addition to the overall antidiscrimination rule, ECOA and Regulation B establish specific requirements and limitations that must be observed in the process of granting credit. The Federal Reserve Board has the responsibility for writing and administering Regulation B.

Loans Covered

An applicant seeking credit primarily for personal, family, or household purposes is covered by both the general antidiscrimination rule and all of the technical provisions of the Act and Regulation B. Loans for business purposes also are subject to the general antidiscrimination rule and the technical provisions, although some exceptions to the technical provision have been provided for business credit (see Business Credit Exceptions).

General Anti-discrimination Rule

The Equal Credit Opportunity Act prohibits a financial institution from discriminating with respect to any aspect of a credit decision on the basis of race, color, religion, national origin, sex, marital status, age (provided the person has the capacity to contract), receipt of income from public assistance programs, and good faith exercise of any rights under the Consumer Credit Protection Act.

Unlawful discrimination also occurs if a financial institution denies an applicant credit because of prohibited considerations concerning the applicant's business associates or persons who will somehow be related to the extension of credit (for example, the race of persons residing in the neighborhood where collateral is located).

The general antidiscrimination rule applies to all applicants and all types of credit. It covers every aspect of the applicant's dealings with the financial institution regarding any extension of credit, including:

1. The gathering and use of information;
2. Procedures for investigation;
3. Standards of creditworthiness;

4. Terms of credit;

5. The furnishing of credit information;

6. The revocation, alteration, or termination of credit; and

7. Collection procedures.

The regulation does not prevent a creditor from determining any pertinent information necessary to evaluate the creditworthiness of an applicant.

Types of Lending Discrimination

Courts have recognized three methods of proving lending discrimination under ECOA:

1. Overt Discrimination

Overt evidence of discrimination occurs when a lender flagrantly discriminates on a prohibited basis. The Federal Reserve's policy statement notes that there is overt evidence of discrimination even when the lender expresses but does not act on a discriminatory preference.

2. Disparate Treatment

Disparate treatment occurs when a lender treats applicants differently on a prohibited basis. Disparate treatment ranges from overt discrimination to more subtle disparities in treatment. There is no required showing that the treatment was motivated by prejudice or conscious intent to discriminate; only a difference in treatment is necessary.

Disparate treatment is most often likely to occur in the treatment of marginally qualified applicants. This disparity is sometimes referred to as the "quality of assistance" provided to an applicant.

3. Disparate Impact

Disparate impact occurs when the lender applies a practice uniformly to all applicants, but the practice has a discriminatory effect on a prohibited basis that is not justified by business necessity. This type of claim may be made for a practice that is uniform on its face, but has a discriminatory result.

Disparate impact claims are frequently proved through statistical analysis. Customary practices will generally not be questioned, but lenders should pay particular attention to standards and practices that are more stringent than is customary.

Equal Credit Opportunity Act

In a February 1995 release, the Department of Justice (DOJ) stated that it would not usually pursue a disparate impact claim unless the impact was significant and there was no "business necessity" for the offending practice or policy. These determinations are made on a case-by-case basis. In addition, DOJ noted that it would focus on practices and patterns of lending discrimination, instead of single discriminatory instances. The only time that DOJ planned to pursue "one instance" pattern or practice was when a particular act provided direct evidence of discrimination, such as an overt statement of discriminatory policy.

Advertising

No financial institution may directly or indirectly engage in any form of advertising that would tend to encourage some types of borrowers and discourage others on a prohibited basis (see also Fair Housing Act).

Applications and Information Gathering

Prescreening tactics that tend to discourage potential applicants are prohibited. This prohibition applies to both written and oral inquiries and applications. Questions must be neutral in nature and of a type applicable to and asked of every applicant desiring the same kind and amount of credit. Lending officers must refrain from asking for prohibited information.

1. Request for Information Concerning a Spouse or Former Spouse

As a general rule, the financial institution may not request information about an applicant's spouse or former spouse except under the following conditions:

a) The nonapplicant spouse will be a user of or joint obligor on the account;

b) The nonapplicant spouse will be contractually liable on the account;

c) The applicant is relying on the spouse's income, at least in part, as a source of repayment;

d) The applicant is relying on alimony, child support, or separate maintenance income as a basis for obtaining credit; or

e) The applicant resides in a community property state, or property on which the applicant is relying on as a basis for repayment of the credit is located in a community property state.

A financial institution may request a list of all accounts upon which the applicant is liable, the name and addresses in which the accounts are carried, and any other names used previously to obtain credit.

2. Request for Information Concerning Marital Status

The financial institution may not ask the applicant's marital status except under the following conditions:

a) The credit transaction is to be secured; or

b) The applicant resides in a community property state or lists assets to support the debt that are located in a community property state.

Only the terms "married," "unmarried," and "separated" may be used to inquire about the applicant's marital status, as permitted.

3. Request for Information Concerning Sex

On the written application, all terms must be neutral as to sex. Courtesy titles indicating sex such as Mr., Mrs., Ms., and Miss may be used, but only if conspicuously designated as optional.

4. Request for Information Concerning Alimony, Child Support, or Separate Maintenance Income

A financial institution may ask if the applicant is receiving alimony, child support, or separate maintenance payments only if it first discloses that such income information need not be revealed unless the applicant wishes to rely on this income for determining creditworthiness.

A financial institution must either ask only for specified income sources (e.g., salary, wages, employment income) or must state that disclosure of alimony, child support, or separate maintenance payments is not required.

5. Request for Information Concerning Childbearing

A financial institution may not request or use information about an applicant's birth control practices or childbearing intentions or capability. The number, ages, and expenses of present dependents may be requested. However, making the assumption that childbearing, or the potential for it, is always associ-

Equal Credit Opportunity Act

ated with a discontinuity in ability to repay is prohibited in an evaluation of creditworthiness.

6. Request for Information Concerning Race, Color, Religion, or National Origin

Financial institutions are prohibited from inquiring about an applicant's race, color, religion, or national origin.

An institution may inquire about the applicant's permanent residence and immigration status in order to determine creditworthiness. However, it may not deny credit arbitrarily to some aliens and not others merely on the grounds that the ones denied are not citizens.

Written Applications

Financial institutions are required to take written applications for loans to purchase or refinance a dwelling (see Fair Housing Act). Creditors may take applications electronically (e.g., the Internet or facsimile) for loans secured by the applicant's home. While written or computerized applications are not required for other types of loans, federal regulations require savings associations to inform inquirers of their right to file a written loan application for any type of credit request.

Application Processing and Evaluation

> An institution may not consider the age of an applicant except to determine legal capacity to contract; to use in an appropriate credit scoring system; or to use in a reverse mortage transaction.

The financial institution may not consider any information it obtains to discriminate on a basis prohibited under Regulation B.

1. Age

The age of the applicant may not be considered (provided the applicant has contractual capacity) unless it is used in an appropriate, empirically derived credit scoring or point system, or in a reverse mortgage transaction.

a) Credit Scoring or Point System

In a credit scoring system, a lender is permitted to consider an applicant's age as long as applicants 62 years or older are treated at least as favorably as applicants who are under 62. If a system scores age by assigning points to an applicant's age, elderly applicants must receive the same or more points as the most favored class of nonelderly applicants.

b) Reverse Mortgage Transaction

A reverse mortgage is a loan, secured by the borrower's home, in which a borrower receives payments from a creditor. Creditors may use age in reverse mortgage transactions to determine the credit line or monthly payment amount that a borrower will receive.

2. Marital Status

A financial institution offering joint credit may not take the applicant's marital status into account in evaluating credit except to the extent necessary to determine rights and remedies for a specific transaction. An institution may not treat joint applicants differently based on the existence, absence, or the likelihood of a marital relationship between the parties.

3. Income

A financial institution must consider income listed by the applicant or spouse including:

a) Income received from a public assistance program;

b) Income derived from annuity, pension, or retirement benefits;

c) Income derived from alimony, child support, or separate maintenance income voluntarily listed by the applicant to support the debt; or

d) Income from part-time employment.

The institution must assess the reliability or unreliability of the applicant's income by analyzing the applicant's actual circumstances, not by analyzing statistical measures derived from a group.

4. Childbearing

A financial institution may not consider statistics or make assumptions concerning the probability that a person like the applicant or the applicant's spouse will have a certain number of children or will cease employment to bear or raise children.

5. Credit History

To the extent credit histories are used in evaluating applications, a financial institution must consider any account reported in the name of both spouses and, on the applicant's request, any account reported in the name of the applicant's spouse that the applicant can demonstrate reflects the applicant's willingness or ability to repay.

If the applicant requests, the financial institution must also consider any information the applicant may present tending to indicate that the credit history of an account reported in both names does not accurately reflect the applicant's ability or willingness to repay.

6. Citizenship

A financial institution may consider whether an applicant is a permanent resident of the United States and the applicant's U.S. immigration status to the extent that this information is necessary to ascertain the financial institution's rights and remedies with respect to repayment.

Appraisals

If the lender appraises any residential property to be used as collateral, the applicant may request a copy of the appraisal report. The lender should furnish a copy promptly after receiving a request and may require reimbursement from the applicant for the cost of the appraisal. This requirement applies whether the loan is for a business or consumer purpose.

A lender may comply with this requirement in one of two ways:

1. Provide a copy of the report to an applicant when the applicant submits a written request. If the lender chooses this method of compliance, it must notify an applicant in writing of the right to receive a copy of an appraisal report. The notice must:

    - Specify that the applicant's request must be in writing;

    - Give the lender's mailing address; and

    - State that the request must be received no later than 90 days after the lender has provided notice of action taken on the application or 90 days after the application is withdrawn.

The lender may give the applicant notice at any time during the application process, but no later than when the lender provides notice of action taken on the application.

2. Routinely provide a copy of the appraisal report to the applicant (whether credit is granted or denied or the application is withdrawn). By regularly

providing a copy of the report, lenders avoid the notification requirements.

Credit Extension

A financial institution may not discriminate on a prohibited basis in the extension or denial of credit.

1. Separate Account

No financial institution may refuse, on the grounds of sex, marital status, or any other prohibited basis, to grant a separate account to a creditworthy applicant. If spouses apply for separate extensions of credit, the accounts must be aggregated to determine finance charges or loan ceilings under state or federal laws.

2. Name on the Account

No financial institution may refuse to allow an applicant to open or maintain an account in a birth-given first name and surname, a spouse's surname or birth-given first name, or a combined surname. The financial institution may require the applicant to use one name consistently in doing business with the financial institution.

3. Change in Name, Employment, or Marital Status

A financial institution may not take the following actions on an existing open-end account on the basis of age, retirement, or a change in marital status:

   a) Require a reapplication (except in limited circumstances);

   b) Change the terms of the account; or

   c) Terminate the account.

The financial institution may require a reapplication in the event of a change in marital status if the credit was based in some part on the income of the spouse, and the income of the person alone does not support the current line of credit. The use of the credit line cannot be denied during the reapplication process.

4. Signature Requirement

A financial institution may not require a signature other than the applicant's if the applicant qualifies for the amount and terms of the credit requested under existing standards of creditworthiness. The financial institution has more latitude in obtaining signatures on necessary security documents than those simply establishing the contractual obligation to repay.

a) *Joint Applicants.* A financial institution may obtain the signature of all joint applicants on both the note and the security instrument. If there is any doubt as to the applicants' intent to be joint borrowers, the loan officer should ask for clarification.

b) *Cosigners.* If the applicant for individual credit cannot solely support the credit, the financial institution may request that the applicant obtain a cosigner or guarantor. The financial institution must be consistent in its request for cosigners among applicants similarly situated. It may not require the applicant's spouse to be the cosigner, and it may not impose requirements on the cosigner that it is prohibited from imposing on the applicant.

c) *Signature of the Applicant's Spouse.* A financial institution may require the spouse's signature if the loan is either based on or secured by property in which the spouse has an ownership interest.

If the applicant resides in a community property state, the financial institution may require the spouse's signature provided the applicant does not possess sufficient separate property or have the power to control or manage enough community property to qualify for the credit request.

d) *Establishment of Credit History.* A financial institution may permit a nonapplicant spouse to voluntarily sign a note and become contractually obligated for repayment as a means of creating a credit history.

e) *Business Credit.* A spouse's signature may be required in a business setting only in the same circumstances that it could in other loans. Business exemptions do not apply to signature requirements.

Creditors may require the personal guarantee of the partners, directors, or officers of a business, even if the business itself was creditworthy. The guarantee would have to be based on the guarantor's relationship with the business and not on a prohibited basis. In certain circumstances, a creditor may also require a disinterested spouse to sign a limited guarantee.

5. Insurance

When insurance is desired by the applicant, information regarding the applicant's age, sex, or marital status may be requested for the purposes of offering insurance.

The financial institution may not deny or terminate credit merely because insurance is unavailable due to the applicant's age.

Notification

Within 30 days of receiving a completed application, the financial institution must notify an applicant of either favorable or adverse action taken on either an oral or written application.

The financial institution can issue a counteroffer (approval conditioned on terms that are not substantially the same as requested by the applicant) within 30 days. If the applicant does not respond within 90 days of the original request, the counteroffer can be retracted.

1. Adverse Action

In general, adverse action means denying (including denying an increase), adversely hanging, or terminating credit. When taking adverse action, the financial institution must give the applicant:

a) A written notice containing a statement of the action taken;

b) A statement describing the applicant's rights under ECOA as prescribed in Regulation B; and

c) Either a statement of specific reasons for the action taken or a disclosure of the applicant's right to receive a statement of the specific reasons, within 30 days of the institution's receipt of a consumer request, provided that the request was made within 60 days of notification of the adverse action.

A creditor that uses a scoring system does not fulfill its statutory responsibility by merely telling the applicant that he or she failed to achieve a passing score. The creditor must disclose the specific reasons for adverse action.

2. Incomplete Applications

As an alternative to the adverse action notification, a financial institution may notify an applicant of information needed on an incomplete application. The written notice must designate a reasonable period of time for the applicant to submit the information. It also must inform the applicant that, unless the information is provided, there will be no further consideration of the application.

If the applicant does not respond within the designated time period, the bank has no obligation to provide further notification.

3. Withdrawn Application

If the financial institution and the applicant agree that the applicant will inquire within 30 days as to the action taken on the application, the institution can consider the application withdrawn if the applicant does not contact the institution within this time period.

4. Multiple Applicants

If two or more persons make a joint application, the notification need only be given to one of the primarily liable applicants.

5. Prequalification and Preapproval Programs

An institution must notify a consumer of an action taken for a prequalification or preapproval request if the institution treats a consumer's request as an application rather than as an inquiry.

An institution treats a request as an inquiry if it provides general information about the application process or about different loan programs. The institution treats a request as an application if, after evaluating information, it decides not to approve the request and communicates that decision to the consumer. For example, when reviewing a request for prequalification, if the institution tells the consumer that it would not approve an application for a mortgage because of a bankruptcy in the consumer's record, the institution has denied an application for credit.

Furnishing Credit Information

Regulation B requires financial institutions that choose to report credit information to designate:

1. Any new account to reflect participation of both spouses if the applicant's spouse is permitted to use or is contractually liable on the account; and

2. Any existing account to reflect participation within 90 days after receiving a written request to do so from one of the spouses.

The financial institution is not required to maintain separate files in the name of each participant on a joint account, but it must be able to report information in the name of each spouse on the account.

Record Retention

The financial institution must maintain the following information:

1. Application form (or, if oral application is made or if preapplication interviews are part of the bank's procedures, any pertinent notation or memorandum made by the loan officer);

2. Written or recorded information used in evaluating an applicant that was not returned to the applicant at the applicant's request;

3. Written or recorded information regarding any action taken concerning an extension of credit, including a copy of the statement of specific reasons for any adverse action (or, if information — or specific reasons — regarding the action taken is furnished orally, any pertinent notation or memorandum made by the loan officer);

4. Information obtained for purposes of governmental credit discrimination monitoring, including the notification of action and statement of specific reasons for adverse action; and any statement of alleged discrimination or other violation submitted by an applicant.

The required documentation must be maintained for 25 months after the date on which the creditor notifies an applicant of any action taken on an application, or of incompleteness, or of an extension of existing credit.

If the creditor is served with, or has actual notice of, any investigation, proceeding, or suit before the end of the 25-month period, the required documentation and all pertinent information must be maintained until there is final disposition of the administrative investigation, enforcement proceeding, or court action.

Indirect Lending Disclosure

When a financial institution purchases indirect paper from a dealer in the regular course of business, it is the responsibility of the financial institution to maintain procedures to determine whether the dealer is complying with the ECOA in all aspects of the credit transaction.

Government Monitoring Information

See Fair Housing Act for discussion of provisions requiring financial institutions to request and maintain information on race, sex, marital status, and age with respect to home purchase and improvement loans to allow the government to monitor compliance with the nondiscrimination laws.

Business Credit Exceptions

Business credit, that is, credit extended for business, commercial, or agricultural purposes, is subject to the general rule under Regulation B that a creditor shall not discriminate against any applicant on any prohibited basis with respect to any aspect of a credit transaction. Financial institutions also are subject to the technical requirements of Regulation B in connection with business credit, with the following exceptions:

1. Requirements to determine whether accounts are shared with spouses in order to furnish credit information are not applicable to business credit.

2. Applicants must be notified within 30 days, orally or in writing, of action taken or of the incompleteness of the application. If the business has gross revenues of $1 million or less, the creditor must inform the applicant in writing, either at the time of application or denial, of the applicant's right to request a statement of reasons for credit denial within 60 days of denial, and to receive that statement within 30 days of such request.

   Regardless of business size, a creditor must provide a written statement of reasons within 30 days of receiving a written request for such statement, provided the request is made within 60 days of the credit denial.

   When an application for business credit is made solely by telephone, compliance with the notice requirements may be satisfied by an oral disclosure of the applicant's right to a statement of reasons for a denial of credit.

3. Any records relating to an application for business credit must be retained for 12 months if the applicant's business has revenues of $1 million or less. Records for businesses with revenues greater than $1 million must be retained for 12 months only if the applicant makes a written request for a statement of credit denial within 60 days of the notification of denial.

Agency Referrals

When the financial supervisory agency has reason to believe that creditors have engaged in a "pattern or practice" of "discouraging or denying" credit applications for a prohibited reason, the matter must be referred to the U.S. Attorney General. The agency may refer other potential ECOA violations to either the U.S. Attorney General or the Secretary of Housing and Urban Development. The agency must notify the applicant when a possible violation is referred to HUD.

Corrective Action

The agencies have judged failure to comply with certain provisions of the ECOA to be particularly serious and, in addition to requiring institutions to be in compliance in the future, generally require retrospective action to correct the condition resulting from the violations. The following types of corrective actions for ECOA violations are suggested by regulators:

- Offering to extend credit if applicants were inappropriately denied, compensating them for any damages, and notifying them of their legal rights;

- Correcting institutional policies that may have contributed to the discrimination;

- Identifying, training, and/or disciplining the employees involved;

- Considering the need for community outreach programs and changes in marketing strategies or loan products to better serve minority segments of the lenders' market; and

- Improving audit and oversight systems to ensure that there is no reoccurrence of the discrimination.

Penalties

In suits by applicants claiming discrimination, Regulation B allows all actual damages and recovery for punitive damages of up to $10,000 in individual lawsuits and up to the lesser of $500,000, or 1 percent of the institution's net worth in class action suits.

References

Laws:

15 U.S.C. 1691 et seq.

Regulations:

12 CFR Part 202 (Reg. B) (FRB)
12 CFR Parts 528 and 571.24 (OTS)

X. Equal Employment Opportunity Act

Introduction and Purpose 106

Agency Guidance 106

Title VII of the Civil Rights Act of 1964 106

Age Discrimination in Employment Act of 1967 107

Equal Pay Act of 1963 107

Executive Orders No. 11141 and No. 11246 108

Rehabilitation Act of 1973 109

Vietnam Era Veterans Readjustment Act of 1974 109

References 109

Introduction and Purpose

Numerous federal statutes and supporting regulations have been enacted to achieve quality of employment opportunity for all persons. The laws aim to achieve this objective by prohibiting employment-related decisions based on specified factors deemed unrelated to job qualifications and, in certain circumstances, by requiring consideration of applicants from some historically employment-disadvantaged groups.

The primary enforcement responsibility for these statutes rests with the Equal Employment Opportunity Commission (EEOC) and the Department of Labor.

Following is a summary of the various Equal Employment Opportunity laws and regulations, including:

1. Title VII of the Civil Rights Act of 1964;
2. Age Discrimination in Employment Act of 1967;
3. Equal Pay Act of 1963;
4. Executive Order No. 11141;
5. Executive Order No. 11246;
6. Rehabilitation Act of 1973; and
7. Vietnam Era Veterans Readjustment Act of 1974.

Agency Guidance

Financial institutions should periodically review their employment practices to assure that they are nondiscriminatory. During the review, financial institutions should consider policies concerning payment of dues on behalf of employees to private clubs that discriminate on the basis of race, sex, religion, color, or national origin. The federal regulatory agencies discourage financial institutions from paying fees or dues for membership on behalf of employees, officers, or directors in private clubs that discriminate on a prohibited basis.

Title VII of the Civil Rights Act of 1964

Title VII prohibits employment-related decisions to be made on the basis of an employee's race, color, sex, religion, or national origin. Institutions cannot discriminate, on a prohibited basis, with regard to:

1. Compensation, terms, conditions, or privileges of employment; and

2. Any action to limit, segregate, or classify applicants or employees that would deprive or tend to deprive any individual of employment opportunities or otherwise affect his or her status as an employee.

Title VII was amended to require employers to treat pregnancy and pregnancy-related medical conditions the same as any other medical disability with respect to all terms and conditions of employment, including employee health benefits.

Charges of unlawful discrimination must be filed with the EEOC within 180 days of the alleged act. However, if the charging party has first filed charges with a state or local fair employment practices agency, the time limit may be extended to 240 days, or to 300 days in some cases.

Remedies may include requiring an employer to end discriminatory practices and systems, and, in some cases, to provide specific "make whole" compensation for victims of discrimination.

Age Discrimination in Employment Act of 1967

The Age Discrimination in Employment Act of 1967 protects employees 40 years of age and older from arbitrary age discrimination in hiring, discharge, pay, promotions, fringe benefits, and other aspects of employment.

The Act requires employers to offer all employees and their spouses 65 years of age and older the same health coverage, under the same conditions, that is offered to employees under age 65. In addition, the Act provides that no seniority system or benefits plan will excuse otherwise prohibited mandatory retirement or a refusal to hire.

A charge of unlawful age discrimination must be filed with the EEOC within two years of the alleged violation (three years if the violation is alleged to be willful). However, to preserve the right to file a private suit in the U.S. District Courts, the charge must be filed with the EEOC within 180 days unless extended under specified conditions.

The EEOC's policy is to seek full and effective relief for each and every victim of employment discrimination, whether it is sought in court or in conciliation agreements reached before litigation.

Equal Pay Act of 1963

The Equal Pay Act of 1963 prohibits:

1. Employers from discriminating on the basis of sex in the payment of

wages to women and men who perform substantially equal work in the same work establishment;

2. Employers from reducing wages of either sex to comply with the law; and

3. Labor organizations from causing employers to violate the law.

The law does not prohibit pay differences based on factors other than sex, such as seniority, merit, or systems that reward actual worker productivity.

Complaints under the Equal Pay Act may be made to the EEOC or the U.S. Department of Labor. Penalties for employer violations of the Equal Pay Act may include payment of back wages, interest, liquidated damages, attorney fees, and court costs. Criminal penalties also may apply.

Executive Orders No. 11141 and No. 11246

These orders prohibit discrimination in employment activities engaged in by federal contractors. The FDIC has successfully defended in court that a financial institution is not a federal contractor merely on the grounds it has deposits insured by the federal government. However, other activities engaged in by a financial institution may qualify it as a federal contractor.

Executive Order No. 11141 prohibits age discrimination in employment activities.

Executive Order No. 11246 requires that:

1. Contracts with the federal government contain an agreement that the contractor will not discriminate against any applicant or any employee because of race, color, religion, sex, or national origin;

2. Affirmative action be taken to insure that applicants and employees are treated without regard to race, color, religion, sex, or national origin;

3. Equal employment opportunity posters be posted in conspicuous places readily visible to employees and applicants;

4. Equal employment opportunity statements be in all recruiting advertisements; and

5. A written affirmative action plan (if more than 50 employees) detail specific steps to guarantee equal employment opportunity and include a table of job classifications in use.

Complaints must be filed with the Department of Labor (Officer of Federal

Rehabilitation Act of 1973

Contract Compliance Programs) within 180 days of the alleged violation unless the time for filing is extended by the director.

The Rehabilitation Act of 1973 prohibits discrimination against physically and mentally handicapped individuals in employment. Special efforts must be made to recruit, employ, train, and promote qualified handicapped persons. An affirmative action program (if more than 50 employees) must set forth policies and procedures to employ and advance qualified handicapped persons.

Complaints must be filed with the Department of Labor (Officer of Federal Contract Compliance Programs) within 180 days of the alleged violation unless the time for filing is extended by the director.

Vietnam Era Veterans Readjustment Act of 1974

The Vietnam Era Veterans Readjustment Act of 1974 prohibits discrimination against disabled veterans and Vietnam era veterans in employment. Special efforts must be made to recruit, employ, train, and promote qualified disabled veterans and Vietnam era veterans.

An affirmative action program (if more than 50 employees) must set forth policies and procedures to employ and advance qualified veterans covered by the Act. Employment opportunities for positions paying under $25,000 annually must be registered with state employment offices.

Complaints must be filed with the Department of Labor (Veteran's Employment Service). Investigation and enforcement are through the Officer of Federal Contract Compliance Programs.

References

Laws:

> 29 U.S.C. 201 et seq.
> 29 U.S.C. 621-634
> 38 U.S.C. 4211 et seq.
> 42 U.S.C. 2000e et seq.
> Executive Order 11141 (Reprinted 5 U.S.C. 3301)
> Executive Order 11246 (Reprinted 42 U.S.C. 2000(e))

Regulations:

12 CFR 528.7 (OTS)
29 CFR Parts 1600-1691 (EEOC)
41 CFR Parts 60-1, 60-25, 60-741 (Office of Federal Contract Compliance Programs)
48 CFR Part 22 (Federal Acquisition Regulations)

XI. Expedited Funds Availability Act

Introduction and Purpose	112
Covered Accounts	112
Next-Day Availability	113
$100 Rule	113
Local Checks	114
Nonlocal Checks	114
Safeguard Exceptions	114
Exception Notice	117
Availability of Exception Deposits	118
Payment of Interest	118
Required Disclosures	118
Additional Disclosures	119
When Funds Are Considered Deposited	120
Record Retention	120
Check Collection	121
Employee Training	121
References	121

112 Consumer Banking Regulatory Handbook

Introduction and Purpose

The Expedited Funds Availability Act was enacted in 1987 and is implemented by Regulation CC (Reg. CC) of the Federal Reserve. Its purpose is to require that depository institutions make funds deposited into transaction accounts available according to specified time schedules and disclose funds availability policies to their customers. The regulation also establishes rules designed to speed the collection and return of unpaid checks.

Covered Accounts

Reg. CC applies to transaction accounts such as demand deposit and NOW accounts. Its provisions govern both consumer and corporate accounts, including the following:

- Accounts from which the holder is permitted to make transfers or withdrawals by negotiable or transferable instruments;

- Payment order of withdrawals;

- Telephone transfers; and

- Electronic payments or other similar means such as the use of ATMs, remote service units, or other electronic devices for the purpose of making payments or transfers to third persons.

The following accounts are not subject to Reg. CC:

- Savings deposits including time deposits and money market deposit accounts;

- Accounts where the holder is a bank;

- Accounts where the holder is an office of a foreign bank that is located outside of the United States; and

- Accounts where the holder is the Treasury of the United States.

For the purposes of Reg. CC, a "business day" is defined as any day excluding Saturdays, Sundays, and legal holidays (standard Federal Reserve holiday schedule). A "banking day" is a business day in which an institution is open for substantially all of its banking activities. Saturday is never a banking day for the purposes of Reg. CC since it is not a business day.

Expedited Funds Availability Act

Next-Day Availability

Cash, electronic payments, and certain check deposits generally must be made available for withdrawal the business day after the banking day on which they were received. Among the covered check deposits requiring next-day availability are cashier's, certified, and teller's checks, government checks (including U.S. Treasury checks, U.S. Postal Service money orders, state and local government checks, and checks drawn on Federal Reserve or Federal Home Loan Banks), and certain "on us" checks (checks drawn on the same institution or a branch of that institution).

Any of these deposits that are:

- Made at a staffed teller station; and

- Deposited into an account held by the payee of the check require next-day availability. U.S. Treasury checks and "on us" checks must receive next-day availability even if the deposit is not made at a staffed teller station. Other next-day check deposits and cash deposits must be available for withdrawal on the second business day after the day of deposit. Funds, including cash and all checks, deposited at nonproprietary ATMs must be made available no later than the fifth business day following the banking day on which the funds are deposited.

For state and local government checks to receive next-day availability, the depository bank must be located in the same state as the governmental unit issuing the check. For "on us" checks to receive next-day availability, the checks must be drawn on a branch of the institution located in the same state or check processing region.

Checks that normally would receive next-day availability are treated as local or nonlocal check deposits if they do not meet all the criteria for next-day availability. U.S. Treasury checks and U.S. Postal Service money orders that do not meet all the requirements for next-day or second-day availability receive funds availability as if they were local checks. Cashier's, certified, teller's, state and local government checks, and checks drawn on the Federal Reserve or Federal Home Loan Banks that do not meet all the requirements receive funds availability as either local or nonlocal checks according to the location of the institution on which they are drawn.

$100 Rule

An institution must make available for withdrawal by the next business day the lesser of $100 or the aggregate amount deposited to all accounts, including individual and joint accounts, held by the same customer on any one banking day. The rule does not apply to deposits received at nonproprietary ATMs.

Local Checks

For remaining deposits, Reg. CC distinguishes between when deposits must be available for check-writing purposes and when they must be available for cash withdrawal. On the second business day, the next $400 of a deposit of local checks (after the first $100 that was made available on the first business day) must be available for cash withdrawal, and the entire deposit for check-writing purposes. On the third business day, the remainder of the deposit must be available for cash withdrawal.

Nonlocal Checks

Deposits of nonlocal checks must be available for check-writing purposes, along with the next $400 for cash withdrawal, by the fifth business day following the day of deposit. The entire deposit must be available for cash withdrawal by the sixth business day. Nonlocal checks are defined as those drawn on financial institutions located in a different Federal Reserve District.

Safeguard Exceptions

The regulation provides six safeguard exceptions that allow institutions to exceed the maximum hold periods in the availability schedules. The exceptions are intended to offer the institution a means of reducing risk based on the size of the deposit, past performance of the depositor, lack of depositor performance history, or belief that the deposit may not be collectible. The exceptions include:

1. New Accounts

An account is considered "new" for the first 30 days after it is established. An account is not considered "new" if each customer on the account had another established account at the bank for at least 30 calendar days. Next-day availability is required for deposits of cash, electronic payments, and the first $5,000 of government, cashier's, certified, teller's, depository, and traveler's checks. Financial institutions are not required to make the first $100 of a day's deposits of local and nonlocal checks, or funds from "on us" checks, available on the next business day.

2. Large Deposits (Over $5,000)

When check deposits exceed $5,000 on any one day, Reg. CC extends hold schedules for the amount in excess of $5,000. To apply the rule, an institution may aggregate deposits made to multiple accounts held by the same customer, even if the customer is not the sole owner of the accounts. This exception does not apply to cash and electronic payments.

3. Redeposited Checks

An institution may delay the availability of funds from a check if the check had been previously deposited and returned unpaid. This exception does not apply to checks that were previously returned unpaid because of a missing endorsement or because the check was postdated when presented.

4. Repeated Overdrafts

If a customer's account has been overdrawn repeatedly during the preceding six months, the institution may delay the availability of funds from check deposits. An account may be considered "repeatedly overdrawn" in one of two ways:

a) If the account has been overdrawn, or would have been overdrawn had checks or other charges been paid, for six or more banking days during the preceding six months; or

b) If the account incurred overdrafts on two banking days within the preceding six-month period and the negative balance in the account is equal to or greater than $5,000 (also applied if the account would have been overdrawn by $5,000 or more had checks or other charges been paid).

5. Reasonable Cause to Doubt Collectibility

This exception may be applied to all checks that ordinarily receive next-day or second-day availability. To trigger this exception, the depository institution must have "reasonable cause" to believe that the check is not collectible and must disclose the basis for the extended hold to the customer.

Reasonable cause may include communication with the paying institution indicating that:

- There has been a stop payment placed on the check;

- There are insufficient funds in the drawer's account to cover the checks; or

- The check will be returned unpaid.

The "reasonable cause" exception also may be invoked because:

- The check is deposited six months after the date of the check (stale date);

- The check is postdated (future date); or

- The depository bank believes that the depositor may be engaged in check kiting.

This exception may not be invoked because of:

- The race or national origin of the depositor; or

- The fact that the paying bank is located in a rural area and the depository bank will not have time to learn of nonpayment of the check before the funds have to be made available under the availability schedules in place.

Whenever this exception is used, the bank must notify the customer, in writing, at the time of deposit. If the deposit is not made in person or the decision to place the hold is based on facts that become known to the institution at a later date, the institution must mail the notice by the business day after the day the deposit is made or the facts become known. The notice must indicate that availability is being delayed and must include the reason that the institution believes the funds are uncollectible.

If the institution invokes this exception and does not inform the customer in writing at the time of the deposit, the institution may not charge the customer any overdraft or returned check fees resulting from the hold if:

- The deposited check is paid by the paying institution; and

- The overdraft or returned check would not have occurred had the depository institution not imposed the reasonable cause hold.

6. Emergency Conditions

Reg. CC also permits institutions to suspend the availability schedules under emergency conditions. Emergency situations include:

- Any interruption of communication facilities;

- Suspension of payments by another depository institution;

- War; or

- Any emergency condition beyond the control of the receiving depository institution.

Whenever this exception is used, the bank must notify the customer in a reasonable form and within a reasonable time, given the circumstances. The notice must include:

- The reason the exception was invoked; and

- The time period in which the funds will be available for withdrawal, unless the bank, in good faith, does not know at the time the notice is given the duration of the emergency condition.

Exception Notice

Whenever an institution invokes one of the safeguard exceptions (other than the new account exception or emergency conditions exception above) to the availability schedule, it must notify the customer in writing. This written requirement may be met by sending an electronic notice, if the customer agrees to such means. The notice must include:

- The customer's account number;

- The date of the deposit;

- The amount of the deposit that will be delayed;

- The reason the exception was invoked; and

- The time period in which the funds will be available for withdrawal (unless unknown, as in an emergency situation).

If the deposit is made at a staffed facility, the written exception notice may be given to the person making the deposit regardless of whether the "depositor" is the customer who holds the account. If the deposit is not made at a staffed facility, the institution may mail the exception notice to the customer not later than the business day following the banking day of deposit.

If, however, the institution discovers a reason to delay the funds subsequent to the time the notice should have been given, it must notify the customer of the hold as soon as possible, but not later than the business day after the facts become known.

An institution may give a one-time notice at or before the time it first determines that the large deposit or redeposited check exception applies to a nonconsumer account.

For consumer and nonconsumer accounts that are subject to the repeated overdraft exception, the one-time notice may be given at the beginning of each time period during which the exception will apply. The FRB has provided model forms for institutions to use in giving the one-time notice.

Availability of Exception Deposits

When a deposit qualifies for a safeguard exception as described above, Reg. CC allows the institution to delay availability for a "reasonable" time beyond the availability schedule. Generally, a "reasonable" period will be considered to be no more than one business day for "on us" checks, five business days for local checks, and six business days for nonlocal checks and cash or checks deposited in nonproprietary ATMs. If an institution extends its availability beyond these time frames, it must be able to prove that such a delay is "reasonable."

Payment of Interest

An institution must begin accruing interest on interest-bearing accounts no later than the business day on which it receives provisional credit for the deposited funds. An institution is permitted to rely on the funds schedule from its Federal Reserve Bank, Federal Home Loan Bank, or correspondent to determine when it receives credit. If availability is delayed beyond what is specified in the schedule, an institution may charge back interest, erroneously paid or accrued, on the basis of that schedule.

An institution also is given the option of accruing interest on checks deposited to all of its interest-bearing accounts based on an average of when the bank receives credit for all checks sent for payment or collection. Consequently, an institution may begin accruing interest on a uniform basis for all interest-bearing accounts without having to track the type of check deposited to each account.

Required Disclosures

An institution must disclose its specific availability policy to its customers. The required disclosures must be clear and conspicuous and in writing. This disclosure must include, as applicable, the following:

- A summary of the institution's availability policy;

- A description of the categories of deposits or checks used by the institution when it delays availability, such as local or nonlocal checks; how to determine the category to which a particular deposit or check belongs; and when each category will be available for withdrawal.

- A description of any of the exceptions that may be invoked by the institution, including the time the deposited funds will generally become available for withdrawal and a statement that the institution will notify the customer if it invokes one of the exceptions; and

- A description of any case-by-case policy of delaying availability that may result in deposited funds being available for withdrawal later than the time periods stated in the institution's availability policy.

An institution that has a policy of making deposited funds available for withdrawal sooner than required may extend the time when funds are available up to the time periods allowed under the regulation on a case-by-case basis. However, it must include the following in its specific policy disclosure:

- A statement that the time when deposited funds are available for withdrawal may be extended in some cases and the latest time that deposited funds will be available for withdrawal;

- A statement that the institution will notify the customer if funds deposited in the customer's account will not be available for withdrawal until after the time periods stated in the institution's availability policy; and

- A statement that customers should ask if they need to know when a particular deposit will be available for withdrawal.

An institution must provide potential customers with the disclosures described above before an account is opened. The disclosures must be in a form the customers may keep.

Additional Disclosures

Deposit Slips

All preprinted deposit slips given to customers must include a notice that deposits may not be available for immediate withdrawal.

Locations Where Employees Accept Consumer Deposits

An institution must post, at a conspicuous place at each location where its employees receive deposits to consumer accounts, a notice that sets forth the time periods applicable to the availability of funds deposited.

Automated Teller Machines

An institution must post or provide a notice at each ATM location that funds deposited in the ATM may not be available for immediate withdrawal. If the institution operates an off-premises ATM from which deposits are removed not more than two times each week, it must disclose at or on the ATM the days in which deposits made at the ATM will be considered received.

Upon Request

An institution must provide a copy of its specific availability policy disclosure to any person who requests it.

Changes in Policy

Thirty days prior to implementation, an institution must send notification of a change in its availability policy to all account holders who are affected adversely by the change. Changes that result in faster availability may be disclosed no later than 30 days after implementation.

When Funds Are Considered Deposited

Funds deposited at a staffed facility, ATM, or contractual branch are considered deposited when received at the staffed facility, ATM, or contractual branch. Funds mailed to the institution are considered deposited on the banking day they are received by the institution. The funds are received by the institution at the time the mail is delivered, even if the mail is initially delivered to a mail room rather than to the check processing area.

Funds deposited at a night depository are considered deposited on the banking day the deposit is removed, and when the contents of the deposit are accessible to the institution for processing.

Funds deposited on a day the institution is closed, or after the cut-off hour, may be considered made on the next banking day. Generally, an institution may establish a cut-off hour of 2:00 or later for receipt of deposits at its main office or branch offices. A cut-off hour of 12:00 noon or later may be established for deposits made to ATMs, contractual branches, lock boxes, night depositories, or other off-premises facilities.

Record Retention

Financial institutions must preserve evidence of compliance with the regulation for at least two years. Generally, an institution is not required to retain records showing that it actually has given disclosures or notices to each customer, but it must maintain evidence demonstrating that its procedures reasonably ensure the customer's receipt of the required disclosures and notices. However, an institution must retain a copy of each notice provided pursuant to its use of the reasonable cause exception as well as a brief description of the facts giving rise to the availability of that exception.

Check Collection

Regulation CC requires paying and returning institutions to return checks using one of two standards:

- *"Two-day/four-day" test.* An institution must return a local check in such a manner that it will reach the depository institution two business days after presentment; a nonlocal check must reach the depository institution within four business days after presentment; or

- *"Forward collection" test.* The paying institution uses transportation methods and institutions for returns that are comparable to those used for forward collection. The paying institution can return checks directly to the depository institution or any institution agreeing to process returns, including the Federal Reserve.

A financial institution also must provide notification of nonpayment if it determines not to pay a check of $2,500 or more, regardless of the channel of collection. The regulation addresses the depository institution's duty to notify its customers that a check is being returned and the paying institution's responsibility for giving notice of nonpayment.

Employee Training

The Expedited Funds Availability Act requires financial institutions to inform each employee who performs duties subject to the Act about its requirements. The Act and regulation also require institutions to establish and maintain procedures designed to assure and monitor employee compliance with such requirements.

References

Laws:

12 U.S.C. 4001 et seq.

Regulations:

12 CFR Part 229 (Reg. CC) (FRB)

XII. Fair Credit Reporting Act

Introduction and Purpose 124

Coverage 124

Transactions Not Covered 124

Disclosures 124

Consumer Reporting Agencies 126

Prescreening 126

Denial of Employment 127

Penalties and Liabilities 127

References 127

Introduction and Purpose

The Fair Credit Reporting Act (FCRA) is designed to regulate the consumer reporting industry, place disclosure obligations on users of consumer reports, and ensure fair, timely, and accurate reporting of credit information.

The purpose of FCRA is to ensure that accurate credit information is used in making credit decisions, that only the information to which the lender is entitled is considered in the loan decision, and that the borrower is informed of the source of any adverse credit information. The Act protects the customer from erroneous information that might be reported by a consumer reporting agency.

Coverage

The Fair Credit Reporting Act covers institutions that are "consumer reporting agencies" as well as those that use information from a consumer reporting agency.

Financial institutions are likely to be subject to FCRA as credit grantors, purchasers of dealer paper, issuers of credit cards, and as employers.

As users of consumer credit information, financial institutions are covered principally by those provisions of FCRA that relate to transactions where consumer credit is denied, or the cost of credit increases partially or wholly on the basis of information from a "consumer report."

Transactions Not Covered

In general, FCRA does not apply to commercial transactions, including transactions that involve agricultural credit.

Disclosures

Identification and Usage

A financial institution must identify itself to the consumer reporting agency and certify that the information it will be requesting will be used as specified in FCRA and for no other purpose. A written blanket certification can be used to cover all inquiries to a particular consumer reporting agency.

Information from a Consumer Reporting Agency

If consumer credit is denied, approved for a lesser amount, or offered at an increased cost partially or wholly on the basis of information from a consumer reporting agency, the institution must disclose, preferably in writing, the following:

1. That information in the report that caused or contributed to the denial or increase in cost; and
2. The name and address of the consumer reporting agency.

Information from a Source Other Than a Consumer Reporting Agency

If consumer credit is denied, approved for a lesser amount, or offered at an increased cost partially or wholly on the basis of information from a source other than a consumer reporting agency, the institution must disclose, preferably in writing, the following:

1. The applicant's right to file a written request for the nature of the information within 60 days of learning of adverse action; or
2. The nature of the information upon which the denial is based.

If a written request is received, the nature of the information must be disclosed in sufficient detail to enable the consumer to evaluate its accuracy. The source of the information need not be, but may be, disclosed.

Comaker, Guarantor, and Surety Disclosures

Disclosure requirements also apply to information from a Consumer Reporting Agency or another source about comakers, guarantors, or sureties. Disclosures should be made to the party to whom they relate.

Other Credit Denial Disclosures

Denial of an overdraft or authorization refusal on a credit card purchase based on information from an outside source also requires a disclosure assuming the information bears upon the consumer's creditworthiness, credit standing, credit capacity, character, general reputation, personal characteristics, or mode of living.

Relationship to Regulation B Disclosures

Disclosures under FCRA are independent from, and cannot be substituted for, those required by Regulation B (see Equal Credit Opportunity Act). They can, however, be made on the same form.

Consumer Reporting Agencies

An institution may become a consumer reporting agency if it regularly furnishes to other individuals or institutions information about a consumer *other than information about the institution's own transactions or experiences.*

Disclosures to Consumers

An institution that is considered a consumer reporting agency must, upon request and proper identification of any consumer, clearly and accurately disclose the following:

- The nature and substance of all information on the consumer (except medical information) in its files at the time of the request;

- The sources of the information (Note: The sources of information acquired solely for preparing an investigative consumer report and actually used for no other purpose need not be disclosed);

- The recipients of any consumer report on the consumer that it has furnished for:

    – Employment purposes within the two-year period preceding the request, and

    – For any other purpose within the six-month period preceding the request.

- The dates, original payees, and amounts of any checks upon which is based any adverse characterization of the consumer, included in the file at the time of the disclosure.

Prescreening

Prescreening is a process by which a financial institution obtains a list from a consumer reporting agency of consumers that meet certain credit-granting criteria that the institution specifies, and then uses that list to solicit those consumers for credit products. Such a prescreened list represents a series of "consumer reports" subject to the FCRA. While not expressly authorized by the FCRA, the Federal Trade Commission has interpreted the Act to permit prescreening if the financial institution makes a firm offer of credit to each consumer whose name appears on the prescreened list.

If an institution issues a firm offer of credit — for example, a preapproved credit card — and based its offer on a prescreened list, it cannot condition or withdraw its offer even if the consumer fails to meet a specified income level or debt-to-income ratio. Once the consumer has accepted the offer of credit, the institution may withdraw the offer of credit only if certain specified circumstances such as foreclosure, filing for bankruptcy, or garnishment occur between the prescreening and the consumer's acceptance of the credit offer.

If the institution uses its own records to prescreen, it does not have to make an offer of credit.

Denial of Employment

An employer must provide disclosure to an applicant for employment who was rejected based on a consumer report.

Penalties and Liabilities

Institutions may be held liable for negligent noncompliance as either users of information or as consumer reporting agencies. In addition to civil liability, punitive damages may be awarded for willful noncompliance. *Any officer or employee of an institution who obtains a credit report under false pretenses will be subject to a penalty of not more than $5,000 or imprisonment for not more than one year, or both.*

References

Laws:

15 U.S.C. 1681 et seq.

Regulations:

16 CFR 600 (FTC)
16 CFR 1.71-1.73 (FTC)

XIII. Fair Debt Collection Practices Act

Introduction and Purpose 130

Activities Covered 130

Activities Not Covered 130

Communications with the Consumer 130

Communications with a Third Party 131

Validation of Debts 132

Prohibited Harassment and Abusive Practices 132

Prohibited Practices Involving Postdated Checks 133

Other Prohibited Practices 134

Multiple Debts 134

Legal Actions by Debt Collectors 134

Furnishing Certain Deceptive Forms 134

References 134

Introduction and Purpose

The Fair Debt Collection Practices Act was designed to eliminate abusive, deceptive, and unfair debt collection practices. While the Act primarily regulates the collection of third-party consumer debts by independent professional debt collectors, banks also are subject to the act to the extent they collect consumer debts for another person or institution.

Activities Covered

The act applies only to the collection of debts incurred by a consumer primarily for personal, family, or household purposes. It does not apply to the collection of corporate debt or to debt owed for business or agricultural purposes.

Under the act, a debt collector is any person who:

1. Regularly collects, or attempts to collect, consumer debts for another person or institution; or
2. Uses some name other than its own when collecting its own consumer debts.

The Supreme Court has ruled that a bank's attorneys are held to the same standards under this Act as other debt collectors.

Activities Not Covered

An institution is *not* a debt collector under the Act when it collects:

1. Another's debts in isolated instances;
2. Its own debts under its own name;
3. Debts it originated and then sold but continues to service;
4. Debts that were not in default when they were obtained;
5. Debts that were obtained as security for a commercial credit transaction (e.g., accounts receivable);
6. Debts incidental to bona fide fiduciary relationships or escrow arrangements; or
7. Debts regularly for other institutions to which it is related by common ownership or corporate control.

Communications with the Consumer

A debt collector may not communicate with a customer under the following conditions:

1. At any unusual time (generally before 8 A.M. or after 9 P.M. in the consumer's time zone) or at any place that is inconvenient to the consumer unless permission is obtained from the consumer or the court;

2. At his or her place of employment if the collector has reason to believe the employer prohibits such communication;

3. If it is known that the consumer has retained an attorney. All contacts must be with that attorney unless the attorney is unresponsive or agrees to allow direct communication with the consumer; or

4. If the consumer refuses, in writing, to pay a debt or requests that the debt collector cease further communication, the collector may advise the customer that the collection effort is being stopped and that certain specified remedies can or will be pursued.

Communications with a Third Party

The only third parties that a debt collector may contact when trying to collect a debt, unless otherwise permitted by the court, are the:

1. Consumer (or consumer's spouse);
2. Consumer's attorney;
3. Consumer reporting agency (if permitted by local law);
4. Creditor;
5. Creditor's attorney; and
6. Debt collector's attorney.

In addition, the debt collector may ask a third party for the consumer's home address, telephone number, and place of employment if unknown to the collector. The collector must reveal his or her name and that he or she is confirming or correcting location information on the consumer. However, unless specifically asked, the debt collector may not name the collection firm or reveal that the consumer owes any debt.

No third party may be contacted more than once unless:

1. The collector believes that the information from the first contact is wrong or incomplete and that the third party has since received better information; or

2. The third party specifically requests additional contact.

Contact with a third party using a postcard, letter, or telegram is allowed only if the envelope or content of the communication does not indicate the nature of the collector's business.

Validation of Debts

If not included in the initial communication and if the consumer has not paid the debt within five days after the initial communication, the following information must be sent to the customer in written form:

1. The amount of the debt;
2. The name of the creditor to whom the debt is owed;
3. Notice that the consumer has 30 days to dispute the debt before it is assumed to be valid;
4. Notice that upon such written dispute, the debt collector will send the consumer a verification of the debt or a copy of any judgment; and
5. Notice that if, within a 30-day period, the consumer makes a written request for the name and address of the original creditor, if different from the current creditor, the debt collector will provide that information.

If within the 30-day period the consumer disputes in writing any portion of the debt or requests the name and address of the original creditor, the collector must stop all collection efforts until the customer has been mailed a copy of the judgment or verification of the debt, or the name and address of the original creditor, as applicable.

Prohibited Harassment and Abusive Practices

A debt collector may not harass, oppress, or abuse any person. Specifically, the collector may not:

1. Use or threaten to use violence or other criminal means to harm the physical person, reputation, or property of any person;
2. Use obscene, profane, or abusive language;
3. Falsely represent or imply that he or she is an attorney, or that communications are from an attorney;
4. Threaten to take any action that is not legal or intended;
5. Falsely represent or imply that the consumer committed a crime or disgrace the consumer in any way;

6. Communicate, or threaten to communicate, false credit information or information that should be known to be false, including not identifying disputed debts as such;

7. Use or distribute written communications made to look like or falsely represented to be documents authorized, issued, or approved by any court, official, or agency of the United States or any state if it would give a false impression of its source, authorization, or approval;

8. Use any false representation or deceptive means to collect or attempt to collect a debt or to obtain information about a customer;

9. Fail to disclose clearly, except as allowed in acquiring location information, that he or she is attempting to collect a debt and that information obtained will be used for that purpose;

10. Falsely represent or imply that accounts have been sold to innocent purchasers;

11. Falsely represent or imply that documents are legal process;

12. Use any name other than the true name of the debt collector's business, company, or organization;

13. Falsely represent or imply that documents are not legal process or do not require action by the consumer; or

14. Falsely represent or imply that he or she operates or is employed by a consumer reporting agency.

Prohibited Practices Involving Postdated Checks

A debt collector may not use the following practices involving postdated checks:

1. Accept any check or other instrument postdated by more than five days, unless he or she notifies the consumer in writing of any intention to deposit the check or instrument. That notice must be made not more than 10 or less than three business days before the date of deposit;

2. Solicit a postdated check or other postdated payment instrument to use as a threat or to institute criminal prosecution; or

3. Deposit or threaten to deposit a postdated instrument before the date on the check or instrument.

Other Prohibited Practices

A debt collector may not use unfair or unconscionable means to collect or attempt to collect a debt, including:

1. Collecting any interest, fee, charge, or expense incidental to the principal obligation unless it was authorized by the original debt agreement or is otherwise permitted by law;

2. Causing communication charges, such as those for collect telephone charges and telegrams, to be made to any person by concealing the true purpose of the communication;

3. Taking or threatening to repossess or disable property when the creditor has no enforceable right to the property or does not intend to do so, or if, under law, the property cannot be taken, repossessed, or disabled; or

4. Use a postcard to contact a customer about a debt.

Multiple Debts

If a consumer owes several debts that are being collected by the same debt collector, payments must be applied according to the consumer's instructions. No payment can be applied to a disputed debt.

Legal Actions by Debt Collectors

A debt collector may file a lawsuit to enforce a security interest in real property only in the judicial district in which the real property is located. Other legal actions may be brought only in the judicial district in which the consumer lives or in which the original contract creating the debt was signed.

Furnishing Certain Deceptive Forms

No one may design, compile, and/or furnish any form that creates the false impression that someone other than the creditor (e.g., a debt collector) is participating in the collection of a debt.

References

Laws:

15 U.S.C. 1692 et seq.

XIV. Fair Housing Act

Introduction and Purpose 136

Activities Covered 136

Prohibited Discriminatory Practices 136

Nondiscriminatory Advertising 137

Nondiscrimination in Prescreening 137

Nondiscrimination in Applications 138

Nondiscrimination in Appraisals and Underwriting 138

Fair Lending Examinations 138

Equal Housing Lender Poster 139

Monitoring Information 139

Loan Application Register Reporting 140

Fair Housing Home Loan Data System 140

References 141

Introduction and Purpose

The Fair Housing Act, Title VIII of the Civil Rights Act of 1968, prohibits various forms of discrimination in connection with (a) the sale or rental of housing, (b) the provision of real estate brokerage services, and (c) the financing of housing.

HUD, the Department of Justice, and the federal financial institutions' regulatory agencies have recently begun emphasizing the importance of complying with the Fair Housing Act. In April 1994, federal regulators adopted a joint policy statement on discrimination in lending. The statement was designed to provide guidance about what agencies consider in determining if lending discrimination exists, and to provide a foundation for future interpretations and rulemaking. Although the policy statement largely restated existing policies and practices, it signaled that fair lending investigations will be pursued with new vigor.

Readers are advised to read this section of the *Handbook* in conjunction with the section on the Equal Credit Opportunity Act, since many of the general prohibitions and remedies are applicable to both sections.

Activities Covered

The Fair Housing Act covers activities in all segments of the real estate industry, including the activities of real estate brokers, builders, apartment owners, sellers, and mortgage lenders. It extends to federally owned and operated dwellings and to dwellings obtained by the use of federally insured loans and grants.

The Act specifically prohibits discriminatory lending practices and applies to any financial institution that makes real estate loans or renders other financial assistance for the purpose of purchasing, constructing, improving, repairing, or maintaining a "dwelling." A dwelling is defined as a residential structure or as vacant land offered for sale for the construction of a residence.

The provisions of the Act also apply to the secondary mortgage market and other purchase and sales transactions involving residential loans and residential-related securities as well as to an institution's managing and marketing of other real estate owned.

Prohibited Discriminatory Practices

The Fair Housing Act makes it unlawful for any lender to discriminate against any person in its "residential real estate-related" activities because of:

- Race;

- Color;

- Religion;
- Sex;
- Handicap;
- Familial status (having one or more children under the age of 18); or
- National origin.

Though primary enforcement authority for the Fair Housing Act is vested in HUD, the financial regulatory agencies have adopted their own nondiscrimination rules that reflect many of the Act's provisions.

A financial institution is prohibited from denying a loan or discriminating in fixing the amount, interest rate, duration, application procedures, or other terms and conditions based on the age or location of the dwelling, or on the race, color, religion, sex, handicap, familial status, marital status, age (provided the person has the capacity to contract), or national origin of:

1. An applicant or joint applicant;
2. Any person associated with the applicant or joint applicant;
3. The present or prospective owners, lessees, tenants, or occupants of the dwelling for which the loan is intended; or
4. The present or prospective owners, lessees, tenants, or occupants of other dwellings in the vicinity of the dwelling for which the loan is intended.

Nondiscriminatory Advertising

No financial institution may directly or indirectly engage in any form of advertising that implies or suggests a policy of discrimination or exclusion as defined above.

Advertisements, other than for savings, must include a facsimile of the "Equal Housing Lender" logotype and legend.

Nondiscrimination in Prescreening

Financial institutions must make every effort to avoid any appearance of discrimination during the pre-screening process. Front-line staff, including receptionists and loan secretaries, should be sure to treat all potential applicants equally. Institutions cannot subtly deter someone from applying for a loan because of race, color, religion, sex, handicap, familial status, or national origin.

Nondiscrimination in Applications

No financial institution may discriminate based on the age or location of the dwelling, or the race, color, etc., of the prospective borrower or other person who:

1. Makes application for any loan or other service;
2. Requests forms or papers to be used to make application for any such loan or other service; or
3. Inquires about the availability of a loan or service.

Each financial institution must inform each inquirer of his or her right to file a written loan application and to receive a copy of the institution's underwriting standards.

Nondiscrimination in Appraisals and Underwriting

No financial institution may use or rely upon an appraisal of a dwelling that the institution knows, or reasonably should know, is discriminatory on the basis of the age or location of the dwelling or race, color, etc., of the applicant.

Each financial institution must have clearly written, nondiscriminatory loan underwriting standards, available to the public upon request, at each of its offices. Each institution must annually review its standards and business practices to ensure equal opportunity in lending.

Fair Lending Examinations

On April 15, 1994, a nine-member interagency task force issued the *Policy Statement on Discrimination in Lending*. The interagency task force included all federal financial institution regulatory agencies, and other federal departments and agencies with jurisdiction over matters of lending discrimination.

The policy statement applies to all lenders, including mortgage brokers, issuers of credit cards, and any other person who extends credit. It clarifies the agencies' positions on certain federal statutes that promote fair lending, including the HMDA, CRA, ECOA, and FH Act. Furthermore, it describes the three methods of proving lending discrimination under these statutes — overt evidence of discrimination, evidence of disparate treatment, and evidence of disparate impact. The interagency task force issued this policy statement for several reasons:

- To provide guidance about what factors the agencies consider in determining if lending discrimination exists;

- To answer questions about how the agencies will respond to lending discrimination and what steps lenders might take to prevent discriminatory practices; and

- To provide a foundation for future interpretations and rulemakings by the agencies.

On April 19, 1995, the OCC released a memorandum, *Fair Lending Guidance: Responsibilities and Timeframes*, to better clarify lending discrimination for examiners and lenders. Together with the April 1994 interagency policy statement, this memorandum provides procedural guidance for addressing violations of the fair lending laws applicable to national banks.

Equal Housing Lender Poster

Each financial institution must prominently post and maintain one or more Equal Housing Lender Posters in the lobby of each of its offices, readily apparent to all persons seeking loans.

The poster must be at least 11" x 14" in size, with easily legible text including a facsimile of the "Equal Housing Lender" logotype and legend, and must contain specific text detailing the basis of discrimination and addresses for submitting complaints.

Financial institutions should post a Spanish language version of the poster in offices serving areas with a substantial Spanish-speaking population.

Monitoring Information

As a means of monitoring compliance with the Fair Housing Act, loan applicants should be requested to provide the following:

1. Race/national origin, using the following categories: American Indian or Alaskan Native, Asian or Pacific Islander, Black, White, Hispanic, Other (Specify);
2. Sex;
3. Marital status, using the categories "married", "unmarried", and "separated"; and
4. Age.

If the applicant(s) chooses not to provide the information or any part of it, that fact should be noted on the monitoring form and the lender must, to the extent possible, on the basis of sight and surname, designate race and sex of each applicant.

Any form used to collect monitoring information must contain a written notice that the information is requested by the federal government to monitor compliance with federal antidiscrimination statutes, and that the lender is required to note race and sex, on the basis of sight and/or surname, if the applicant(s) chooses not to do so.

Institutions should note that discriminatory mortgage lending can exist despite the adoption of clear policies against such discrimination. Statistical analysis, the most commonly used method to detect discriminatory lending practices, may show a pattern or practice of disparate treatment of loan applications, which could subject lenders to prosecution.

Loan Application Register Reporting

For examination purposes, each financial institution must maintain at each of its decision centers a current, readily accessible loan application register reporting applications for the following loan types:

1. One- to four-family home purchase loans;
2. Refinance of home purchase loans;
3. Multifamily loans;
4. Mobile home loans; and
5. Home improvement loans.

Home equity loans secured by one- to four-family dwellings may, at the option of the financial institution, be included on the loan application register if the primary loan purpose is stated as home improvement.

See the HMDA section of this *Handbook* for a thorough explanation of these reporting requirements and procedures.

Fair Housing Home Loan Data System

To assist in determining compliance with the Fair Housing Act, the OCC developed the Fair Housing Home Loan Data System (FHHLDS). National banks that are not subject to HMDA requirements must collect and retain lending information under the FHHLDS. These banks are to update records quarterly in order to assist examiners in determining if they consistently apply loan approval and pricing policies. For the purpose of this regulation, a home loan includes any real estate loan for the purchase, permanent financing for construction, or the refinancing of residential real property that the applicant intends to occupy as a principal residence.

Recognizing that duplication of information occurs under FHHLDS and the Home Mortgage Disclosure Act, the OCC does not require FHHLDS reporting for national banks subject to HMDA. Instead, these banks are to maintain information on the HMDA Loan/Application Registers and are responsible for updating these records on a quarterly basis. See the Home Mortgage Disclosure Act section of this *Handbook* for additional information on HMDA reporting.

References

Laws:

42 U.S.C. 2000d et seq.
42 U.S.C. 3601 et seq.
2 U.S.C. 3631

Regulations:

12 CFR Part 27 (OCC)
12 CFR Part 338 (FDIC)
12 CFR Parts 528 and 571.24 (OTS)
24 CFR 100 (HUD)

XV. Flood Disaster Protection Act

Introduction and Purpose 144

NFIP Programs 144

Mandatory Flood Insurance 145

Regulatory Requirements 145

Loans Covered 145

Community Requirements 147

Insurance Coverage 147

Notification Requirements 147

Mortgage Portfolio Protection 149

Recordkeeping Requirements 150

References 151

Introduction and Purpose

The Flood Disaster Protection Act of 1973 (FDPA), which was significantly revised by the National Flood Insurance Reform Act of 1994, provides for federally subsidized flood insurance to property owners located in flood hazard areas. Rather than providing federal disaster relief money after a flood occurs, Congress elected to make flood insurance available at a more reasonable cost.

The Act created the Federal Emergency Management Agency (FEMA) to administer the program. FEMA identifies communities with Special Flood Hazard Areas (SFHA), issues maps for those areas, helps communities qualify for the National Flood Insurance Program (NFIP), and assists them in adopting flood plain management requirements.

When a community elects to participate in the NFIP, FEMA performs a study of the community and creates Flood Hazard Boundary Maps that are used to determine if properties are located in areas having special flood or mudslide hazards. FEMA also produces Flood Insurance Rate Maps that divide the community by degrees of probability of flood hazard. These maps identify flood boundaries, elevations, and insurance risk zones.

NFIP Programs

The NFIP is divided into two phases: the emergency program and the regular program. Communities first entering the NFIP are eligible for the emergency program. Under this program, insurance is provided for lower limits of coverage (first layer) at federally subsidized rates on eligible buildings.

After FEMA performs a detailed study of the community and issues Flood Insurance Rate Maps, the community enters the regular program. This program provides full insurance coverage (first and second layers) in addition to flood management requirements for the area.

Compliance Guidelines

When making loans secured by improved real estate, institutions should follow these steps to ensure compliance with flood insurance requirements:

1. Determine flood hazard status of property;
2. Notify the borrower in writing if flood insurance is required;
3. Obtain the borrower's signed acknowledgment of receipt of notice;

4. Require evidence from the borrower of appropriate flood insurance prior to closing;

5. Monitor insurance coverage on property throughout the term of loan;

6. Keep required records.

Mandatory Flood Insurance

Federally regulated financial institutions may not originate, refinance, increase, extend, or renew any loan secured by improved real estate or a manufactured home that is on a permanent foundation if:

1. The property securing the loan is located in an area FEMA has identified as having special flood or mudslide hazards (A&V zones carry mandatory coverage requirements);

2. The community participates in NFIP; and

3. The property securing the loan does not have flood insurance.

The flood insurance requirement does not apply to:

- State-owned property that is insured in a manner satisfactory to FEMA; and

- Loans with an original outstanding balance of $5,000 or less and with a repayment term of one year or less.

The FDPA also prohibits using federal financial assistance (including loans, grants, and guarantees from the Federal Housing Authority or VA mortgage insurance) for the acquisition or construction of a structure in a special flood hazard area unless the community participates in the NFIP and flood insurance has been purchased.

Regulatory Requirements

Financial regulatory agencies must ensure that financial institutions:

1. Do not make loans secured by uninsured real estate or manufactured homes located in an SFHA if the community participates in the NFIP;

2. Notify the purchaser or lessee of the availability of federal disaster relief assistance and of the possibility of flood hazards before making flood-related loans; and

3. Comply with recordkeeping requirements.

Loans Covered

The NFIP covers any loan secured by improved real estate located, or to be located, in an area identified by FEMA as having special flood hazards. The program covers residential or commercial loans regardless of purpose, including:

- Building construction loans (only after the building has walls and a roof);

- Condominiums or townhouses that may be separately owned;

- High-rise condominiums with common ownership;

- Other types of residential, industrial, commercial, and agricultural buildings;

- Mobile and manufactured homes that are affixed to a permanent site; and

- Dealers' inventories of mobile homes on foundations.

Standard Flood Hazard Determination Form

The Standard Flood Hazard Determination Form (FEMA Form 81-93), produced by the Federal Emergency Management Agency, must be used by lenders to verify whether the property securing the loan is located in an SFHA and must be retained for the period of time the bank owns the loan. On the form lenders must identify the:

- Type of flood-risk zone in which the property is located;

- Complete map and panel numbers of the property;

- Community identification number and NFIP participation status; and

- Date of map used for SFHA determination.

If the property is not located in an SFHA, the form requires a statement to this effect along with the complete map and panel numbers of the property. If the property is not located in an SFHA and complete map and panel numbers are unavailable because the property is not in a participating NFIP community, or because no map exists for the area, the form requires a statement of the reason for the lack of the information.

Information Provider Must Guarantee Accuracy

An institution may use a third party to make the determinations required on the form only if the third party guarantees the accuracy of the information. An institution should ensure that the information provider can support a guarantee in case a determination is inaccurate.

Community Requirements

In order to receive federal funds in the event of flooding, flood-prone communities are required to:

1. Participate in the NFIP; and
2. Take land use measures — such as restricting building in high-risk areas or establishing building codes requiring the elevation of certain structures — in order to have flood insurance available.

Insurance Coverage

If flood insurance is required, the policy must cover the amount of the loan or the maximum amount available under the NFIP, whichever is less.

Effective Dates of Policies

A new flood insurance policy purchased in connection with the making, increasing, extension, or renewal of a loan, or a policy purchased within one year of a property's new designation within an SFHA, is effective immediately. Coverage under all other new policies is effective 30 days after the application is completed and initial premiums paid.

Notification Requirements

Special Flood Hazards

When a loan is secured by property located in a community that has been identified as a special flood hazard, regardless of whether the community is participating in the NFIP, a financial institution is required to mail or deliver a written notice to the borrower at least 10 days before closing. This notice must state:

1. That the property is located in a flood hazard area;
2. A description of the flood insurance purchase requirements;
3. That flood insurance coverage is available under NFIP or private insurers, where applicable; and
4. Whether federal disaster relief assistance will be available for such prop-

erty in the event of damage caused by flooding in a federally declared disaster area.

In addition, the financial institution must obtain a written acknowledgment from the borrower that the property is located in an SFHA, and that the borrower has received the mandatory notice regarding federal disaster relief assistance.

Change of Service

Under revised regulations, the federal regulatory agencies must require an institution to notify FEMA in writing or electronically (if electronic transmission is satisfactory to FEMA) of:

- The servicer of a loan;

- Any change in the servicer (within 60 days of the effective date of the change).

Continuing Notice Obligation

If, at origination or at any time during the term of a covered loan, an institution determines that a property subject to the mandatory flood insurance requirement is uninsured or has inadequate coverage, the institution must notify the borrower that the borrower should obtain, at the borrower's expense, the required amount of flood insurance.

If a community is rezoned and a property is no longer within an SFHA, to avoid potential lawsuits from borrowers, an institution should send a relief notice to the borrower stating that the borrower is no longer required by law to have flood insurance. An institution may wish to advise that the borrower is eligible for lower rates and encourage the borrower to maintain flood insurance coverage. An institution should refrain from stating that flood insurance is no longer needed.

Institution's Obligation to Purchase Flood Insurance

If the borrower fails to purchase the required insurance within 45 days after notification, the institution must purchase the required amount of insurance and may charge the borrower for the premiums and fees incurred in purchasing the insurance. This requirement applies to all loans outstanding on or made after September 23, 1994.

Fees for Determining Applicability of Insurance Requirements

An institution may pass along to the borrower the costs of determining whether the improvement is located in a flood hazard area if the determination:

- Is made in connection with a making, increasing, extending, or renewing of the loan that is initiated by the borrower;

- Reflects the Director of FEMA's revision or updating of floodplain areas or flood-risk zones;

- Reflects the Director of FEMA's publication of a notice that:

  – Affects the area in which the building or mobile home securing the loan is located; or

  – Requires a determination whether the building or mobile home securing the loan is located in a special flood hazard area; or

- Results in the purchase of flood insurance coverage by the bank or its servicer on behalf of the borrower; or

An institution may charge this fee to a purchaser or transferee where the loan is sold or transferred.

Escrow of Flood Insurance Payments

The National Flood Insurance Reform Act of 1994 required the federal regulatory agencies to establish flood insurance escrow regulations. Under these regulations, any institution that requires escrowing of taxes, fees, or other charges relating to a covered loan on residential improved real estate or on a mobile home will also have to require escrowing of all flood insurance premiums and fees. This requirement applies to all covered loans made, increased, extended, or renewed after September 23, 1995.

Mortgage Portfolio Protection

The Mortgage Portfolio Protection Plan (MPPP) assists lenders in bringing their portfolios into compliance with FDPA. Specifically, the MPPP allows mortgage lenders to insure properties that are part of its mortgage portfolio and that remain uninsured through the property owner's (mortgagor's) inaction.

The MPPP cannot be used in connection with new loan transactions. It can be used only in connection with a lender's effort to bring its mortgage portfolio into compliance with flood insurance purchase requirements. The program does not replace the disclosures required or the evidence that flood insurance has been purchased, if applicable, prior to loan origination.

In order to qualify for MPPP membership the property must meet the following guidelines:

- The property must be located in a special flood hazard area;

- The property must be located in a community that participates in the NFIP; and

- The lender must provide the property owner with notice of the lack of insurance, but the owner (mortgagor) has failed to respond.

Recordkeeping Requirements

Institutions must maintain sufficient records to indicate the method used to determine whether loans require flood insurance. At a minimum, such records must include:

- Copies of official maps, including the date and complete panel number of the FEMA map used to determine whether the improved real estate or manufactured home is located in or out of a flood hazard zone;

- If applicable, a statement that FEMA has not published a flood insurance map for the community in which the improved real estate or manufactured home is located;

- Written statements in each file indicating that a flood determination was performed and the result; and

- Copies of any written contracts between the bank and the independent vendors or appraisers performing flood assessments.

Institutions should also retain appropriate documents whenever the property securing the loan is in a flood hazard area. Such documents may include:

- Copies of notices provided to the borrower;

- The borrower's written acknowledgment of receipt; and

- If the purchase requirement applies, a copy of the flood insurance policy. Banks may choose to indicate on their records that property securing a particular loan is not in a flood hazard area.

An institution may charge the borrower fees associated with a portfolio review only where the property was found to be uninsured or underinsured *and* the institution purchased flood insurance as a result.

Penalties

When an institution's primary regulator finds that an institution has engaged in a pattern or practice of noncompliance with the flood insurance purchase or notification requirements, the regulator must assess a civil money penalty of up to $350 for each violation to a maximum of $100,000 per institution per year. The civil money penalties are separate from other available civil or criminal liability.

References

Laws:

    42 U.S.C. 4012a et seq.

Regulations:

    12 CFR Part 22 (OCC)
    12 CFR 208.8(e) (FRB)
    12 CFR Part 339 (FDIC)
    12 CFR 572 (OTS)

XVI. Home Mortgage Disclosure Act

Introduction and Purpose 154

Nondepository Mortgage Lenders 154

Loans Covered 155

Loans Excluded 155

Data Reporting under the Community Reinvestment Act 155

Home Equity Lines of Credit 156

Loan/Application Register 156

Data Accuracy 156

Submission of Register 157

Disclosure Statement 157

Public Notice 157

References 157

Introduction and Purpose

The Home Mortgage Disclosure Act (HMDA) and the Federal Reserve Board's Regulation C apply to all financial institutions that originate or purchase mortgage loans, have total assets greater than $28 million, and have a home or branch office in a Metropolitan Statistical Area (MSA).

The purpose of HMDA is to provide the public with information that shows how a financial institution is serving the housing credit needs of the neighborhoods and communities in which it is located. This information also is intended to assist public officials in distributing public sector investments so as to attract private sector investments to needed areas.

HMDA deals solely with recordkeeping and disclosure; it does not prohibit or require any loan activity by financial institutions.

The FFIEC has issued a statement that "HMDA compliance will be emphasized in examinations." All regulatory agencies will be informed about late, inaccurate, or incomplete HMDA statements. Each agency's examination staffs have been instructed during the next examination to follow up any deficiencies in an institution's HMDA reporting noted in the previous examination. Institutions also should be aware that regulators have announced plans to scrutinize HMDA reports for signs of lending discrimination and follow with targeted exams for particular institutions or geographic areas where apparent disparities appear.

Nondepository Mortgage Lenders

A nondepository mortgage lending institution is covered by HMDA if the nondepository lender has a home office or branch office in an MSA, and for the previous calendar year:

1. The institution's assets (in conjunction with any parent institution) exceeded $28 million, *or* the institution (independent of its parent) originated 100 or more home purchase loans (including refinancings); and

2. The institution's home purchase loan originations (including refinancings) equaled or exceeded 10 percent of its total loan origination volume, measured in dollars.

For the purposes of HMDA reporting, uninsured U.S. branches and agencies of foreign banks, and Edge Act and Agreement Corporations are considered to be nondepository mortgage lenders. If such institutions meet or exceed the thresholds above, they must comply with HMDA reporting requirements.

Home Mortgage Disclosure Act 155

Loans Covered

HMDA requires each reporting institution to collect data regarding applications for, and originations and purchases of, home purchase loans (including refinancings) and home improvement loans for each calendar year. It covers:

1. Home purchase loans, defined to include any loan or refinancing secured by and made for the purpose of purchasing a "dwelling." A dwelling includes both one- to four-family and multifamily properties including condominiums, cooperatives, and mobile and manufactured homes;

2. Home improvement loans, defined to include any loan or refinancing whether secured or unsecured that is used for repairing, remodeling, or rehabilitating a dwelling or the real property on which it is located, and that is recorded on the bank's books as a home improvement loan;

3. Loans insured or guaranteed by the Federal Housing Administration (FHA), Farmers Home Administration (FmHA), or the Veterans Administration (VA); and

4. Loans intended to be sold to the Federal National Mortgage Association (FNMA) or the Federal Home Loan Mortgage Corporation (FHLMC).

Loans Excluded

Excluded loans include:

1. Loans made or purchased in a fiduciary capacity;
2. Loans on unimproved land;
3. Construction loans and temporary financing;
4. Purchases of interests in a pool of mortgages; and
5. Purchases solely of servicing rights.

Data Reporting under the Community Reinvestment Act

As of January 1, 1996, a bank or savings association that has assets of at least $250 million, or is a subsidiary of a holding company with total banking and thrift assets of at least $1 billion, must collect and report geographic data for *all* loans and applications relating to property, including those outside MSAs. See the Community Reinvestment Act section in this *Handbook*.

Home Equity Lines of Credit

If a home equity line of credit is obtained for home improvement, then the lender has the option of including the loan in the report. If the line of credit is obtained for other purposes, then it should not be reported in the Loan/Application Register.

Loan/Application Register

The data required to be maintained must be compiled quarterly in a Loan/Application Register format as prescribed in Regulation C. The Loan/Application Register reports the following data:

1. A number for the loan or loan application and the date the application was received;

2. Type, amount, and purpose of the loan or application;

3. Whether the property is owner occupied;

4. Whether or not the loan was made, the date of the decision, and the reason for denial (if applicable);

5. Applicant or borrower's race, sex, and gross annual income (collection of this information is optional for purchased loans);

6. If the loan or application relates to property in an MSA where the institution has a home or branch office, then the institution is required to report the MSA number, state, and county codes, and the 1990 Census tract number;

7. The type of entity purchasing each loan that the association originates and sells during the same calendar year; and

8. Additional fair lending information required by the federal regulatory agencies. This additional information appears in Section II. It includes data relating to: CRA delineated community, marital status, age, purchase price, appraised value, loan-to-value ratio, interest rate, year built, and maturity.

Data Accuracy

In the past few years, regulatory authorities have frequently stressed the importance of filing accurate HMDA data. The filing of inaccurate HMDA data may subject an institution to civil money penalties.

Submission of Register

Each financial institution must submit a copy of the Loan/Application Register to the appropriate federal regulatory agency by March 1 following the year for which the data were compiled. Depending on the number of entries, the data must be on either one automated machine-readable form or on two nonautomated copies that are typed or computer printed. The institution must retain a copy for its records for at least three years, and must make a modified version of the loan application register available to the public.

Disclosure Statement

The Register is forwarded by the regulatory agencies to the Federal Financial Institutions Examination Council (FFIEC), which then prepares and sends to each financial institution a disclosure statement and various reports showing lending patterns for that institution. The disclosure statement and reports are expected to be returned to financial institutions by October following the year for which the data were compiled.

The financial institution is required to make the disclosure statement available to the public at its home office (full disclosure statement) and in at least one branch office in each MSA (may be limited to data in that MSA) no later than three days after it receives the statement.

Public Notice

A public notice about the availability of its disclosure statement shall be posted in the lobbies of the home office and each branch located in an MSA.

References

Laws:

12 U.S.C. 2801 et seq.

Regulations:

12 CFR Part 203 (Reg. C) (FRB)

XVII. Homeownership Counseling

Introduction and Purpose 160

Covered Financial Institutions 160

Covered Loans 160

Notice Requirement 160

Exceptions 161

References 161

Introduction and Purpose

Under the Housing and Urban Development Act of 1968, all financial institutions that service conventional mortgage loans and loans insured by the Department of Housing and Urban Development (HUD) must notify delinquent borrowers of the availability of homeownership counseling services provided by the creditor and by HUD-approved counseling organizations. In addition the notification must be given to certain first-time homebuyers at the time of application.

Covered Financial Institutions

The notice requirement applies to any financial institution servicing a home loan for itself or for another entity. The servicer of a loan, not the owner, is obligated to provide the required notice. But an institution that merely receives mortgage payments for another entity and does not contact homeowners to discuss delinquent accounts would not be considered a "servicer" and thus would not be required to send the notice.

Covered Loans

The homeownership counseling procedures apply to those loans secured by a mortgage or lien on a borrower's principal residence. Residence is defined as a "one-family dwelling," which includes a condominium unit, a manufactured home, or cooperative unit. It includes home equity loans secured by the mortgagor's principal residence.

Notice Requirement

A financial institution must notify a homeowner who fails to pay any amount by the date the amount is due, under the terms of the home loan, of the availability of homeownership counseling. The notification must be made within 45 days from the date the payment was due. HUD recommends that the notice be included in the creditor's first communication with the homeowner regarding deficiency.

The notification must advise the delinquent homeowner of:

- The availability of any homeownership counseling services offered by the financial institution; *and* either

- The HUD-approved nonprofit homeownership counseling organizations, or

- The HUD toll-free telephone number (800-733-3238) through which the homeowner can obtain a list of HUD-approved counseling organizations that serve the homeowner's residential area.

In addition to delinquent homeowners, banks must provide the notification to applicants who are "eligible" first-time home buyers, defined as an individual, displaced homemaker, or single parent that has had no or limited ownership in a principal residence during the prior three-year period. To be eligible the mortgage must involve a principal obligation in excess of 97 percent of the appraised value of the property and be insured through HUD's Mutual Mortgage Insurance Fund, which is administered by FHA.

HUD issues, and periodically updates, a listing of all HUD-approved home ownership counseling agencies.

Though financial institutions are not themselves required to provide homeownership counseling services, such institutions are encouraged to employ counselors who at least meet the standards set by HUD.

Exceptions

The notice requirement does not apply to loans:

- Guaranteed by the Department of Veterans Affairs; or

- For which the amount overdue is paid before the expiration of the 45-day period.

References

Laws:

12 U.S.C. 1701(x)

XVIII. Interest on Deposits

Introduction and Purpose 164

Deposit Account Requirements 164

Premiums 166

Finders' and Brokers' Fees 167

Advertising 167

References 167

Introduction and Purpose

Before 1980, the payment and advertising of interest on deposits, including interest ceilings, were governed primarily by the Federal Reserve Board's Regulation Q. The Depository Institutions Deregulation and Monetary Control Act of 1980 provided for an orderly phase-out of interest rate ceilings under the direction of the Depository Institutions Deregulation Committee (DIDC). On March 31, 1986, the authority of DIDC expired as did all interest rate ceiling authority. Effective April 1, 1986, banks and thrifts may pay interest on all deposit accounts, other than demand accounts, at whatever rates they choose, consistent with their deposit contracts and with safety and soundness considerations.

Deposit Account Requirements

Despite the elimination of interest ceilings, deposit accounts are still subject to certain limitations.

Regular Savings (Passbook) Account

There are no specific limitations on passbook savings accounts except that an insured financial institution must reserve the right to require at least seven days' notice prior to withdrawal.

Fixed-Term (Certificate) Account

A certificate account must have a term of at least seven days and provide the following disclosures:

1. The rate or anticipated rate of earnings to be paid, the basis, frequency, extent, and limits of any variation in the rate over the term of the account, and the dates or frequency at which earnings are distributable;

2. The amount of the account and the date of issuance;

3. The minimum term and minimum balance requirement;

4. Any provisions limiting the right of the holder to make additions to the account or to withdraw all or any portion of the account prior to its maturity;

5. The penalty or penalties for withdrawal prior to expiration of the term;

6. Any provisions relating to redemption, call, or repurchase;

7. Any provisions relating to a renewal when the term expires;

8. Any provisions relating to earnings after expiration of the term or any renewal period; and

9. Any provisions converting the rate of return on the certificate account to another rate of return whenever any minimum balance requirement may cease to be met.

The depositor may not withdraw funds within six days after deposit unless the withdrawn funds are subject to an early withdrawal penalty of at least seven days' simple interest. There are several exceptions to the minimum penalty provisions, including:

- When the time deposit represents funds contracted to an IRA or Keogh account and the person has reached age 59 1/2 or is disabled; and

- When a time deposit is withdrawn within 10 days after a specified maturity date, even though the deposit contract provided for automatic renewal at the maturity date.

A financial institution *may* impose penalties for withdrawal of any portion of a certificate account prior to maturity except:

1. After the death of an account owner, if the withdrawal is requested by any other owner of the account or by the authorized representative of the decedent's estate; or

2. After an account owner is determined to be legally incompetent, if the account was issued before the date of such determination and not extended or renewed after that date.

Money Market Deposit Account

Money market deposit accounts (MMDAs) can be made available to any depositor, including individuals, corporations, government entities, and non-profit organizations. The financial institution must reserve the right to require seven days' notice prior to withdrawal.

Depositors are restricted to no more than *six* transfers per calendar month or statement cycle of at least four weeks. These transfers may be by preauthorized, automatic, telephonic, or data transmission agreement, order, or instruction to another account of the depositor at the same institution, to the institution itself, or to a third party.

No more than *three* of these transfers may be by check, draft, debit card, or similar order made by the depositor and payable to third parties.

The depositor may make *unlimited* transfers for:

1. Repaying loans and associated expenses at the financial institution;

2. Interaccount transfers in person or at an ATM from the MMDA account to accounts of the same account holder at the same association; and

3. Cash or check withdrawals made in person, by mail, messenger, ATM, or telephone (via check mailed to the depositor).

In order to ensure compliance, the financial institution must:

1. Prevent transfers in excess of the limitations; or

2. Adopt procedures to monitor transfers after the fact, including steps to ensure that the excessive transfers do not continue. If excessive transfers persist, the institution must either restrict access or transfer the funds into another type of account.

Negotiable Order of Withdrawal (NOW) Account

NOW accounts may only be held by:

1. One or more individuals (including unincorporated businesses and non-profit organizations);

2. Government entities depositing public funds; and

3. Nonprofit organizations, as defined by the Internal Revenue Code.

The institution must reserve the right to require at least seven days' notice prior to withdrawal or transfer of any funds in the account. The institution is authorized to permit withdrawals by negotiable or transferable instruments for the purpose of making transfers to third parties.

Checking (Demand Deposit) Account

Financial institutions are authorized to issue demand deposit accounts to any person, but are restricted from paying interest on these accounts.

Premiums

Premiums on demand deposit accounts in the form of merchandise, credit, or cash will not be considered the payment of interest if:

1. The premium is given to the holder of a demand deposit only upon opening a new account or adding to, or renewing, an existing demand account;

2. The premium is unrelated to the amount or the duration of a deposit;

3. No more than two premiums per account are given within a 12-month period;

4. The value, or total cost, of the premium does not exceed $10 for deposits of less than $5,000 or $20 for deposits of $5,000 or more (averaging of values or costs of premiums is not permitted);

5. Funds are not solicited on the basis that the funds will be divided into several accounts for the purpose of paying the depositor more than two premiums within a 12-month period on the solicited funds; and

6. The financial institution maintains and makes available all necessary information in its files to enable an examiner to determine its compliance with these requirements.

Finders' and Brokers' Fees

Finders' and brokers' fees will not be considered to be payment of interest on the account if:

1. The fee is a bonus in cash or merchandise to the insured institution's employees for participation in an account drive, contest, or other incentive plan where the bonus is based on the total amount of deposits solicited; or

2. The fee is paid to a bona fide broker (one who is principally engaged in the business of brokering deposits), there is a written agreement between the broker and the insured institution, and an officer of the broker gives written certification that no portion of the fee paid is directly or indirectly passed on to the depositor.

Financial institutions may choose to absorb expenses incurred by providing a normal banking function or by waiving fees in connection with these services without their being considered as a payment of interest on the account.

Advertising

Advertisements, announcements, and solicitations made by a financial institution, or by others on its behalf, relating to interest or dividends paid on an account are governed by the Truth in Savings Act and by Regulation DD. See the Truth in Savings Act section of this *Handbook*.

References

Laws:

12 U.S.C. 1464(b)(1)
12 U.S.C. 1832

Regulations:

    12 CFR Part 204 (Reg. D) (FRB)
    12 CFR Part 217 (Reg. Q) (FRB)
    12 CFR Parts 545, 561, and 563 (OTS)

XIX. Real Estate Settlement Procedures Act

Introduction and Purpose 171

Transactions Covered 171

Transactions Not Covered 171

Dealer Loans 172

Special Information Booklet 172

Good Faith Estimate of Settlement Costs 173

Uniform Settlement Statement (HUD-1 and HUD-1A) 174

Escrow Accounts 175

Escrow Statements 176

    Initial Statement 176

    Annual Statement 177

Referral Fees and Kickbacks 177

Affiliated Business Arrangements 178

Title Companies 179

Identity of Person Receiving Benefit 179

Fees for Required Statements 179

Mortgage Servicing 180

    Disclosures at Time of Application 180

    Disclosures at Time of Transfer 180

    Payments During the Transfer Period 181

    Error Resolution 181

FHA Loan Prepayment Disclosures 182

References 182

Real Estate Settlement Procedures Act 171

Introduction and Purpose

The Real Estate Settlement Procedures Act (RESPA) was enacted in 1974 and is implemented by Regulation X of the Department of Housing and Urban Development (HUD). Its purpose is to provide borrowers with pertinent and timely disclosures regarding the nature and costs of the real estate settlement process. It also protects borrowers against abusive practices such as kickbacks or unearned fees, and places limitations upon the use of escrow accounts.

Transactions Covered

RESPA generally applies to any mortgage loan, including refinancings, originated by a financial institution that is secured by a first or subordinate lien on residential property (including condominiums and mobile homes) intended for occupancy by one to four families.

Transactions Not Covered

RESPA does not apply to:

1. *Property of 25 Acres or More.* A loan on property of 25 or more acres;

2. *Business Purpose Loans.* An extension of credit primarily for business, commercial, or agricultural purposes. Any transaction in which one or more persons, acting in an individual capacity, places a lien on a one- to four-family residential property, whether used for occupancy or investment, is not considered a business purpose loan;

3. *Temporary Financing.* Temporary financing includes bridge loans, swing loans, and construction loans. This exemption does not cover construction loans used to finance construction of new or rehabilitated one- to four-family residential property if the loan is used as, or may be converted to, a permanent loan to finance the purchase by the first user;

4. *Vacant Land.* Loans secured by vacant land or unimproved property. Lenders must ensure the loan proceeds are not intended to finance construction of a one- to four-family residential structure on the property within two years from settlement of the loan;

5. *Assumption without Lender Approval.* Any assumption in which the lender does not have the express right to approve a subsequent person as the borrower on an existing federally related mortgage loan;

6. *Loan Conversions.* Any modification of a federally related mortgage loan to different terms that are consistent with provisions of the original mort-

gage instrument, as long as a new note is not required, even if the lender charges an additional fee for the conversion (conversions from a fixed-term obligation to a variable rate obligation are not exempt); and

7. *Secondary Market Transactions.* Bona fide transfers of loan obligations in the secondary mortgage market.

Dealer Loans

A "dealer," for RESPA purposes, means either a seller, contractor, or supplier of goods or services in connection with a home improvement loan, or someone in the business of manufactured home retail sales in connection with a manufactured home loan.

A "dealer loan" is an arrangement in which a dealer assists a borrower in obtaining a loan from the funding lender, the dealer's interests are assigned to the funding lender, and the dealer receives the net proceeds of the loan. A loan or advance by a dealer in which the dealer does not assign its interest and receives the loan payments directly would not be a covered RESPA transaction, unless the dealer is otherwise classified as a lender under RESPA.

For the initial assignment of a dealer loan, the funding lender is responsible for:

- Assuring that the necessary disclosures (such as the good faith estimate) are made in a timely manner, by either the lender or the dealer; and

- Assuring that a HUD-1 or HUD-1A settlement statement is used.

Special Information Booklet

The lender must give the HUD special information booklet, *Settlement Costs and You*, to the applicant for every loan covered by RESPA, except refinancings. The booklet provides prospective home buyers with information concerning the mechanics, costs, and normal lending practices involved in home financing.

The lender must give the booklet to the applicant when the application is received, or must mail the booklet within *three business days of receipt of the application*. Only one copy per loan is required, even if there are multiple borrowers. If the lender denies the loan before the end of the three-business-day period, the lender need not provide the booklet to the borrower.

For home equity lines of credit, the lender must provide the borrower with a copy of "When Your Home Is On the Line: What You Should Know About

Home Equity Lines of Credit" or any successor brochure issued by the Federal Reserve.

Good Faith Estimate of Settlement Costs

The lender must provide the applicant a good faith estimate of the amount or range of each settlement charge the borrower is likely to incur at or before settlement based upon common practice in the locality of the mortgaged property. Although they need not exactly match the actual charges, it is important that the lender be able to justify all of its estimates.

The lender must give the good faith estimate to the applicant when the application is received, or must mail the statement within *three business days*. If the lender denies the loan before the end of the three-business-day period, the lender need not provide a good faith estimate to the borrower. The good faith estimate disclosures must be made on a HUD-approved form that includes the name of the lender.

For "no cost" or "no point" loans, charges paid to third-party settlement cost providers should be shown as P.O.C. (Paid Outside of Closing) on the estimate and on the HUD-1 or HUD-1A. Otherwise no distinction is made between charges paid at, or outside of, closing.

If the lender requires the use of a particular provider of a settlement service, other than the lender's own employees, and also requires the borrower to pay any portion of the cost of such service, then the good faith estimate disclosure must:

- Clearly state that the provider is required and that the estimate is based on the charges of the designated provider;

- Give the name, address, and telephone number of each provider; and

- Describe the nature of any relationship between each such provider and lender.

A relationship exists if the provider is an associate of the lender, has maintained an account with the lender, or had an outstanding loan or credit arrangement with the lender within the last 12 months; or the lender has repeatedly used or required borrowers to use the services of the provider within the last 12 months.

An associate of a lender includes:

- A spouse, parent, or child of the lender;

- A corporate parent, subsidiary, or affiliate of the lender;

- An employer, officer, director, partner, franchisor, or franchisee of the lender; or

- Anyone who has an agreement with the lender that permits them to benefit financially from the referral of settlement services.

If the lender will choose from a list of less than five providers, it must list all of the providers and use the highest cost of the listed providers and the estimated cost for the service. If the lender will choose from a list of five or more required providers, it must:

- State that the required provider is unknown at this time, but will be chosen from a pool of approved providers;

- Use the highest cost from the pool of providers as the estimated cost for the service; and

- Disclose the specific provider used and the actual cost on the HUD-1.

Except for a provider that is the lender's chosen attorney, credit reporting agency, or appraiser, the lender may not require the use of a provider, if the lender is in an affiliated relationship with the settlement service provider. (See Affiliated Business Arrangements in this section.)

For home equity loans, the lender will be considered in compliance with the good faith estimate disclosure requirements if it provides to the consumer the disclosures required by the Truth in Lending Act. (See Home Equity Lines of Credit under the Truth in Lending Act Section in this *Handbook*.)

Uniform Settlement Statement (HUD-1 and HUD-1A)

A closing statement must be provided to the buyer on *a Uniform Settlement Statement (HUD-1)* form that clearly itemizes all charges imposed on the buyer and seller in conjunction with the settlement, including information about payments to and from any escrow account during the first 12 months. Alternatively, for transactions in which there is a borrower and no seller, such as refinancing or subordinate lien loans, the institution may use the HUD-1A. Note that a HUD-1 or HUD-1A is not required if the borrower is not required to pay any settlement charges or adjustments, or only pays a fixed settlement charge determined at the time of application.

The financial institution is required to make available the HUD-1 or HUD-1A to the borrower one day prior to settlement if requested by the borrower.

The completed HUD-1 or HUD-1A must be mailed or delivered to the borrower and seller, or their agents, at or before settlement. When the borrower waives such delivery, does not attend settlement, or no meeting is required, the completed HUD-1 or HUD-1A is to be mailed to both buyer and seller as soon as practical after settlement.

The financial institution must retain the HUD-1 or HUD-1A for five years, unless it disposes of its interest in the property and does not service the mortgage.

Escrow Accounts

A lender may not require a borrower to have on deposit in an escrow account any amount in excess of the amount that is sufficient to pay taxes, insurance premiums, or other charges incurred up to the date of the first full mortgage payment, plus a reserve in the amount of one-sixth of such charges to be paid during the following 12 months. Any monthly escrow payment cannot be larger than one-twelfth of the amount anticipated to be paid for such charges during the following 12 months, plus the amount necessary to maintain a balance not to exceed one-sixth of the amount of charges to be paid during that period (two months reserve).

Lenders are required to conduct an escrow account analysis both at the creation of an escrow account and at the end of each escrow account computation year. The initial analysis will determine the initial amount the borrower will deposit into the escrow account and the amount of the borrower's periodic payments into the account. The annual analysis will determine whether a surplus, shortage, or deficiency exists in the escrow account.

Where there is a surplus (the current escrow balance exceeds the target balance for the next year), the lender must, depending on the amount, either refund the surplus amount or credit it against next year's escrow payments. Where there is a shortage (the current escrow balance falls short of the target balance for next year), the lender may, depending on the amount, do nothing, allow the borrower to repay the shortage over 12 months, or require the borrower to pay the entire shortage within 30 days. Where there is a deficiency (the lender has had to advance funds to the account in order to make a required disbursement), the lender may, depending on the size of the deficiency, do nothing, allow the borrower to repay the deficiency in two or more payments over a period of up to 12 months, or require the borrower to pay the deficiency within 30 days. A lender is required to notify the borrower at least once during the year if there is a shortage or deficiency in the escrow account.

In the past, lenders and servicers used one of two methods to analyze escrow accounts: the single-item accounting method or the aggregate accounting method. The single-item accounting method requires that each item to be paid out of escrow be accounted for separately. Under this method, payments could be required from borrowers to make a payment on a single escrow item regardless of the fact that the escrow account as a whole had sufficient funds to pay the bill that was due. As a result, consumer advocates and several states' attorneys general criticized the single-item method for resulting in overescrowing, i.e., the average balance of the escrow account being higher than necessary.

Lenders and servicers are now required to use aggregate accounting for escrow accounts on all mortgage loans closed after May 24, 1995. Under the aggregate accounting method, lenders are required to consider what is available in the escrow account as a whole when accounting for the payment of escrowed items. There is a three-year phase-in period for the aggregate accounting method for any mortgage loans with a settlement date before May 24, 1995. Any mortgage servicer using the single-item accounting method on loans settled before that date may continue to do so until May 24, 1998.

The financial institution must make timely payments out of the borrower's escrow account, using a disbursement date on or before the earlier of the deadline to take advantage of discounts, if available, or the deadline to avoid a penalty.

Escrow Statements

Initial Statement

At settlement, or within 45 days after establishing an escrow account, the servicer must send the borrower an initial escrow account statement. The initial statement must include:

- The amount of the borrower's monthly mortgage payment;

- The portion of the monthly payment going into the escrow account;

- An itemization of the estimated taxes, insurance premiums, and other charges that the servicer reasonably anticipates to be paid from the escrow account during the year and the estimated date of those disbursements;

- The amount selected by the servicer as the account cushion; and

- A trial running balance for the account.

HUD has issued an approved format for use by servicers in providing the initial disclosure.

Annual Statement

For each escrow account, a servicer must submit an annual escrow account statement to the borrower within 30 days of the completion of the account computation year. The servicer must conduct an escrow account analysis before sending the annual statement to the borrower.

The annual statement must include the following information:

1. The borrower's current monthly payment and the portion of the monthly payment going into the escrow account;
2. The amount of the past year's monthly mortgage payment and the portion of that payment that went into the escrow account;
3. The total amount paid into the escrow account during the past year;
4. The total amount paid out of the escrow account for each separately identified escrow item;
5. The balance in the escrow account at the end of the period;
6. An explanation of how any surplus is being handled by the servicer;
7. An explanation of how any shortage or deficiency is to be paid by the borrower; and
8. If applicable, the reason(s) why the estimated low monthly balance was not reached.

Referral Fees and Kickbacks

Fees and payments for services related to settlement of a loan covered by RESPA are limited to reasonable fees for services actually performed. No fee, kickback, or other thing of value may be given to or received by anyone for referring settlement services. In addition, no fee or payment for settlement services may be split with anyone not actually providing the service.

RESPA does not prohibit payment of reasonable compensation for services actually performed. It also does not prohibit normal promotional or educational activities that are not conditioned on the referral of business.

Employer-Employee Referral Fee Exemption

In 1992, HUD issued a rule that provided a general exemption from the RESPA prohibition of referral fees for a payment by an employer to its own employees for any referrals of settlement services. HUD issued a new rule in June 1996 that withdraws the general employer-employee exemption. Under the new rule, employers may make referral payments to their own employees only if:

- The employee is a managerial employee, and the payment is not calculated as a multiple of the number or value of referrals;

- The employee does not perform settlement services in any transaction, the employee provides the customer with a controlled business arrangement disclosure prior to the referral, and the referral is to an affiliate of the employer; or

- The payment is to the employer's own employees for generating business for the employer.

Note that while an employer may, within these guidelines, compensate its employees for referrals to the employer's affiliates, the affiliate may not compensate the employee or otherwise reimburse the employer for paying the referral fee (see section of this chapter on Affiliated Business Arrangements). In May 1997, HUD proposed to broaden the exemption from the RESPA prohibition of fees paid to employees for referring customers to an affiliated company. Under the proposal referrals would be exempt if:

- Both the company for which the employee works and the affiliate to which the customer is referred offer the "same category" of mortgage service;

- The employee discloses the affiliate business arrangement; and

- The referring employee does not perform any other kind of mortgage service in the same transaction.

Affiliated Business Arrangements

An affiliated business arrangement is an arrangement in which a lender has either an affiliate relationship with, or ownership interest of more than 1 percent in, a provider of settlement services and directly or indirectly refers settlement business to that provider or affirmatively influences the selection of the provider.

Affiliated business arrangements will not be considered a violation of RESPA's prohibition on referral fees or kickbacks so long as the following requirements are met:

- A written statement is provided at the time of referral to the user of the settlement service disclosing the nature of the relationship between the provider of the settlement service and the party making the referral and the estimated charge or range of charges generally imposed by the service provider (the disclosure must be in the format of the HUD-issued model disclosure form);

- The person making the referral may not require the use of the affiliated business settlement service provider; and

- The only thing of value that may be received for the referral, other than reasonable compensation otherwise permitted under RESPA, is a return on ownership interest or franchise relationship.

As mentioned above, it is permissible for a bank, or other entity, to pay certain of its own employees for referrals to affiliated businesses for settlement services. It is, however, impermissible for a controlled business affiliate to compensate the bank or the bank employee directly or indirectly for the referral of such settlement services.

Title Companies

In the event that the financial institution holds legal title to the property being sold, the financial institution (seller) is prohibited from requiring borrowers, either directly or indirectly, to use a specific title company.

Identity of Person Receiving Benefit

Each financial institution is required to know the identity of the person receiving the beneficial interest of any mortgage loan made to an agent, trustee, nominee, or other person acting in a "fiduciary capacity."

Fees for Required Statements

No fee may be charged for the preparation and distribution of the HUD-1 or HUD-1A settlement statement, or any required escrow account statements.

Mortgage Servicing

Disclosures at Time of Application

Mortgage lenders must disclose to each applicant certain information about the lender's policy on loan servicing. To assist lenders, HUD has issued a model disclosure statement. The disclosure statement must include information regarding:

- Whether the loan servicing may be transferred to another institution;

- The percentage of loans, to the nearest quartile, transferred in each of the past three years;

- The best available estimate of the percentage of loans, to the nearest quartile, for which servicing may be assigned, sold, or transferred during the next year;

- A summary of the information that will be provided at the time a loan is transferred, including information on servicing procedures, transfer practices, and requirements; and

- A summary of the institution's duty to respond to borrower inquiries.

The disclosure statement also must include a signed acknowledgment that the applicant has read and understands the disclosure. A loan may not be funded unless a signed acknowledgment is in the file. A copy of the signed acknowledgment must be maintained for five years.

Except for the acknowledgment portion, it is not mandatory that the language in the model disclosure statement be used exactly as written by HUD, but all required information must be included in any substitute statement.

Disclosures at Time of Transfer

When a servicer transfers a loan, *both* the current servicer and the new servicer must make the following disclosures to the borrower:

- The date upon which the first payment will be due to the new servicer;

- The name and address of the new servicer;

- Toll-free or collect call telephone numbers for the current servicer and the new servicer that the borrower may use to make inquiries relating to the transfer;

- The date after which the current servicer will stop accepting payments;

- The effect of the transfer on the availability or terms of any optional insurance; and

- A statement that the transfer does not affect the obligations or rights of the borrower under the security instruments.

The current servicer must deliver the disclosure at least 15 days before the effective date of the transfer, defined as the date on which the first payment is due at the address of the new servicer. The new servicer's notice must be delivered no later than 15 days after the effective date of the transfer. Both notices may be combined if the disclosure is sent 15 days before the effective date of the transfer.

If the information about the transfer is known when the loan closes, the lender may fully satisfy its disclosure requirement by providing a notice as part of the closing documents.

Payments During the Transfer Period

During the first 60 days after the effective date of the transfer of loan servicing, the borrower may deliver payments to either the current or new servicer. If the payment is received by either servicer on a timely basis, the borrower may not be assessed late charges or reported as delinquent to a credit reporting agency.

Error Resolution

A loan servicer is required to respond to a borrower's written request to correct an error or to obtain information. The servicer has 20 days after receipt of the borrower's letter to provide a written acknowledgment of receipt of the letter or take the requested action. The servicer has 60 days after receipt of the letter to:

1. Correct the account and notify the borrower in writing of the correction;

2. After conducting an investigation, provide a written explanation as to why the account is correct; or

3. Provide the requested information or an explanation as to why the information is unavailable.

In each case, the response must include the name and telephone number of a person or department that the borrower may contact for additional information. During the 60-day resolution period, the servicer may not report to any consumer reporting agency a delinquency based on the amount in dispute.

FHA Loan Prepayment Disclosures

There is another disclosure requirement that, while not technically a part of RESPA requirements, may be made with other disclosures. The Cranston-Gonzalez National Affordable Housing Act requires that, for all FHA mortgages closed on or after August 22, 1991, the financial institution must provide to the borrower, at or before closing, a statement disclosing the requirements that the borrower must fulfill upon a prepayment of the mortgage in order to avoid the accrual of any interest on the FHA mortgage after the prepayment date.

The regulation also makes mandatory the issuance of an annual statement to all borrowers holding FHA loans that states:

1. The amount of outstanding principal balance of the loan; and
2. Any requirements the borrower must fulfill to avoid the accrual of additional interest on the mortgage loan in the event of prepayment.

HUD has published a mandatory format to be used in both the initial and annual disclosures.

References

Laws:

12 U.S.C. 2601 et seq.

Regulations:

24 CFR 3500 (Reg. X) (HUD)

XX. Right to Financial Privacy Act

Introduction and Purpose 184

Customer Protection 184

Customer Notice 184

Agency Certification 184

Exceptions to Certificate of Compliance Requirement 185

Form of Request 185

Bank Compliance 186

Recordkeeping Requirements 186

Reimbursement 187

Exceptions to Reimbursement 187

Civil Liability 187

Customer Notice Prohibited 188

References 188

Introduction and Purpose

The Right to Financial Privacy Act (RFPA), together with provisions of the U.S. criminal code, regulate the circumstances under which a financial institution is permitted to furnish customer information or records to federal authorities, such as the FBI, DEA, and federal courts. In most instances, a financial institution, before providing customer information, must be assured that the customer is aware of the request. That assurance usually is in the form of a certification from the requesting federal agency. In some instances, such as a court subpoena issued in a pending civil case, no customer notice or agency certification is necessary. In a few instances, such as a subpoena from a grand jury investigating a possible crime against a financial institution, customer notice is prohibited.

Customer Protection

The RFPA protects the privacy of each financial institution "customer." A customer is a person (or representative of that person) who uses any service provided by a financial institution, or for whom an institution acts as fiduciary. The definition excludes corporations and partnerships of six or more persons; their records are not protected by RFPA.

Customer Notice

RFPA generally requires a federal government authority to notify a customer of its request or demand to a bank to provide information or records about that customer. The law specifies the content and timing of the government's notice, so that the customer may have an opportunity to seek a court order preventing the requested disclosure. RFPA also specifies the circumstances under which the government authority may delay or avoid a customer notice.

Agency Certification

A federal government authority seeking the customer information or records from the institution generally must certify to the institution in writing that the authority has complied with RFPA. The institution may rely on this certification without determining itself whether a customer notice was required and, if so, properly given. Unless an exception applies, the bank should always request a certificate of compliance from the investigating agency in order to protect itself from privacy claims by a customer.

Exceptions to Certificate of Compliance Requirement

RFPA does not apply, and, therefore, certification and customer notification are not required, if:

1. The customer's records are requested by a federal financial agency in the exercise of its supervisory, regulatory, liquidation, lending, or monetary functions, including regular examinations and investigations of consumer complaints;

2. An institution submits copies of financial records to a court or agency to perfect a lien, prove a claim in bankruptcy proceedings, or collect a debt for itself or as a fiduciary;

3. An institution releases financial records not individually identifiable with a particular customer;

4. The customer and the requesting federal agency are parties to litigation and records are requested under a subpoena issued by a court under the Federal Rules of Civil or Criminal Procedure or by an administrative law judge in a formal adjudicatory proceeding;

5. A subpoena or court order requests information or records for a federal grand jury under specific procedures in conjunction with grand jury proceedings;

6. An institution is notifying law enforcement officials about what it believes may be a violation of the law, and includes only the name or other information identifying the person or account involved;

7. The IRS requests records in accordance with the Internal Revenue Code;

8. The records are requested by the U.S. General Accounting Office (GAO) for an authorized proceeding or audit directed at a federal agency;

9. Federal statutes or regulations require the information to be reported;

10. An institution is informing appropriate law enforcement officials about possible crimes against a financial institution or supervisory agency by an insider or borrower; or

11. A customer's name and address is provided to the Social Security Administration or the Railroad Retirement Board.

Form of Request

When a financial institution receives a federal authority's request or demand in one of the following forms for customer information, the institution also must receive the authority's certificate of RFPA compliance before releasing the information:

1. A written authorization, signed and dated by the customer within the last three months, that identifies the records being sought and the reasons that such records are being requested, and outlining the customer's rights under RFPA;

2. An administrative subpoena or summons;

3. A search warrant;

4. A judicial subpoena;

5. A formal written request by a federal government agency that is issued under regulations put into effect by the head of the requesting agency or department; or

6. A request from a government authority conducting foreign intelligence or counterintelligence activities or from the Secret Service in conducting its protective activities.

Bank Compliance

Financial institutions should begin collecting the requested information when the request, summons, subpoena, or demand is received. Upon receipt of the authority's certificate of RFPA compliance, only the records or information specifically requested should be released.

Financial institutions should not be overzealous in volunteering information beyond that requested by subpoena. Doing so may violate various state laws and subject the institution to potential liability.

A financial institution should designate one person to be in charge of all subpoenas. This individual should be very familiar with the RFPA.

Recordkeeping Requirements

A financial institution should record each instance when it has disclosed a customer's records to a federal authority in accordance with the customer's written authorization. Records also must be kept if information is provided in connection with a federal authority's assistance to a customer in the form of a loan, loan guaranty, or loan insurance agreement.

All records should include:

1. The date the financial information was released;

2. The name of the federal authority requesting such information; and

3. Identification of all records disclosed to the requestor.

Institutions also should maintain copies of all administrative and judicial subpoenas, search warrants, and formal written requests submitted by federal government agencies or departments along with the required written certification. Generally, these records should be provided to the customer upon request or for inspection unless otherwise prohibited.

Reimbursement

A financial institution may charge for assembling records requested by federal authorities. The amount that may be charged, and the conditions under which the charges may be made, are contained in the Federal Reserve's Regulation S. Reasonably necessary costs that are directly incurred while searching for, reproducing, or transporting books, papers, records, or other data requested are covered. An itemized invoice should be submitted to the requesting agency at the same time that the information is delivered to the agency.

Exceptions to Reimbursement

Expenses incurred by the institution that are not reimbursable include work connected with:

1. Government loan programs;

2. Federal civil or criminal litigation;

3. Certain administrative subpoenas issued by administrative law judges;

4. GAO requests for gathering information such as records furnished in connection with government loan programs; or

5. Some IRS summonses.

Civil Liability

A violation of RFPA gives the affected customer a right to sue an institution for monetary damages and attorneys' fees. Good faith reliance on a government authority's certification of RFPA compliance or on a belief that the information related to a possible crime against an institution or a supervisory agency by an insider or borrower is a valid defense to such a suit.

Customer Notice Prohibited

In the following instances, an institution and its employees are prohibited from informing a customer that his or her records have been requested or provided:

1. The request was made by a government authority conducting foreign intelligence or counterintelligence activities, or by the Secret Service in conducting its protective activities;

2. A court has ordered that a grand jury subpoena not be disclosed; or

3. A subpoena is received from a grand jury investigating a possible crime against a financial institution or involving money laundering or drug offenses. WARNING: In this instance, disclosure of the subpoena or of releasing records in response to the subpoena may be prosecuted as an obstruction of justice.

References

Laws:

    12 U.S.C. 3401 et seq.

Regulations:

    12 CFR Part 219 (Reg. S) (FRB)

XXI. Truth in Lending Act

Introduction and Purpose 191

The 1997 Amendments 191

TILA Scope 191

Credit to a "Consumer" 192

Exempt Transactions 192

Credit Categories 193

Disclosures 193

Calculations and Estimates 194

Subsequent Events 194

Refinancing 194

Multiple Creditors or Consumers 195

Annual Percentage Rate (APR) 195

APR Accuracy Tolerances 196

Finance Charge 197

Charges Included 197

Charges Excluded 199

Open-End Credit 200

Issuance of Credit Cards 201

Application Disclosures 201

Initial Disclosures 202

Variable Rate Information 203

Subsequent Disclosures 203

Periodic Statement Disclosures	203
Additional Disclosures	204
Transaction Identification	204
Crediting Payments and Refunds	205
Cardholder Liability	206
Prohibition of Offsets	206
Cardholder Claims and Defenses	207
Billing Error Resolution	207
Advertising Credit Terms	208
Home Equity Lines of Credit	209
HELC Disclosures	209
HELC Variable Rates	210
Restrictions on HELCs	211
Closed-End Credit	212
Disclosures	212
Required Disclosures	213
High-Rate/High-Fee Mortgages	217
Reverse Mortgages	219
Right of Rescission	220
Violation Reimbursement	222
Institution's Liability	222
References	222

Introduction and Purpose

The Truth in Lending Act (TILA) was enacted in 1968 as a part of the Consumer Credit Protection Act. The act has been amended several times by Congress, most recently in 1997. It is implemented by the Federal Reserve's Regulation Z.

TILA's purpose is to assure meaningful disclosure of credit terms so that consumers will be able to compare more readily the various terms available and avoid the uninformed use of credit. It also is designed to protect the consumer against inaccurate and unfair credit billing and credit card practices.

Financial institutions are required to maintain evidence of compliance with all of the requirements of Regulation Z for at least two years after the date required for action to be taken or disclosures to be furnished.

The 1997 Amendments

In March 1997, the Board published revisions to the official staff commentary to Regulation Z. This commentary applies and interprets the requirements of Regulation Z. The revisions provide guidance on issues relating to the treatment of certain fees paid in connection with mortgage loans, address new tolerances for accuracy in disclosing the amount of the finance charge, and discuss the treatment of debt cancellation agreements. These revisions became effective February 28, 1997.

TILA Scope

TILA contains provisions regulating the following:

- Disclosures that a creditor is required to furnish to the consumer any time the creditor extends consumer credit;

- Form and content of advertisements for consumer credit;

- Issuance of credit cards;

- Consumer's liability for the unauthorized use of credit cards; and

- Consumer rights against a creditor.

In general, TILA and Regulation Z apply to each individual or business that offers or extends credit when four conditions are met:

1. The credit is offered or extended to consumers who are U.S. residents (including resident aliens);

2. Consumer credit was offered more than 25 times during the previous year, more than five times for transactions secured by a dwelling, or more than once for high-rate/high-fee mortgages (or once for high-rate/high-fee mortgages through a broker);

3. The credit is subject to a finance charge or is payable by a written agreement in more than four installments; and

4. The credit is primarily for personal, family, or household purposes.

Credit to a "Consumer"

For most purposes, TILA protects only a "consumer" who is a natural person to whom credit is offered or extended. A natural person who guarantees any debt by giving a security interest in his or her principal dwelling is a "consumer" for the limited purpose of receiving a right of rescission and notice of that right. Any credit card holder — including a business or other organization — is a "consumer" for the limited purposes of TILA restrictions on the issuance of a credit card and on liability of the holder for a card's unauthorized use.

Exempt Transactions

Transactions that do not have a consumer purpose are generally exempt from all requirements of TILA. Transactions not subject to TILA and Regulation Z include:

- Credit extended to any business or organization, including corporations, partnerships, associations, trusts, unions, and government agencies;

- Credit extended primarily for a business, commercial, or agricultural purpose;

- Credit extended to government agencies or instrumentalities;

- Credit over $25,000 not secured by real property or a dwelling;

- Credit involving certain public utility services if the charge for the service, delayed payment, or any discounts for prompt payment are filed with or regulated by any government unit;

- Transactions in securities or commodities accounts if the credit is extended by a broker dealer registered with the Securities and Exchange Commission or the Commodity Futures Trading Commission;

- An installment agreement for the purchase of home fuels in which no finance charge is imposed;

- Certain student loans; and

- Loans for non owner-occupied rental housing.

Credit Categories

Regulation Z divides covered consumer credit transactions into two categories: open-end credit and closed-end credit.

1. Open-end credit is consumer credit extended under a plan in which the financial institution:

   a) Reasonably expects repeated transactions;

   b) May impose a finance charge from time to time on the outstanding unpaid balance; and

   c) Generally makes credit extensions available to the consumer during the term of the plan (up to any limit set by the financial institution) to the extent that any outstanding balance is repaid.

   The financial institution must make required disclosures before the account is actually used and with each billing statement.

2. Closed-end credit is all consumer credit not included as open-end credit. This includes residential mortgage and installment credit contracts, including purchased dealer paper. With closed-end credit, the borrower must receive the required disclosure before the loan is consummated.

Disclosures

Required disclosures must be made in writing, and in a form that the consumer may keep. They should not be buried in fine print and should be visible without undue searching, and they must be phrased to communicate information clearly and effectively. The disclosures must reflect the terms of the legal obligation between the consumer and the financial institution.

In addition, whenever Regulation Z requires the terms "finance charge" or "annual percentage rate" to be disclosed with a corresponding amount or percentage rate, then these disclosures should attract the consumer's attention more readily than other required terminology. This may be accomplished by using larger or bolder type, underlining, marking with an asterisk, or printing in colored ink.

Calculations and Estimates

Disclosed amounts and percentages should reflect the terms of the customer's legal obligation to the institution. The institution must, at a minimum, use generally accepted calculation tools, although it need not invest in a sophisticated computer program to make a particular type of calculation. If required information is unknown or not reasonably available at the time the disclosures are made, Regulation Z permits the institution to estimate the information. All estimates must be identified as such and must be based on the best information reasonably available.

Subsequent Events

All disclosures required under Regulation Z must be made on the assumption that the terms and conditions of the legal contract will be carried out as agreed. However, subsequent events can lead to the original disclosures becoming inaccurate. Examples include when a customer makes late payments, fails to insure the property, or pays the loan off early. Inaccuracies in original disclosures are not violations if they are attributable to such subsequent occurrences. As a result, additional disclosures are not required unless certain annual percentage rate inaccuracies, refinancings, or residential mortgage transaction assumptions are involved.

Refinancing

Under TILA, institutions must provide consumers with a complete set of new disclosures whenever a refinancing occurs. Under Regulation Z, a "refinancing" occurs whenever a new obligation completely replaces the earlier one. Refinancings may involve the consolidation of several existing obligations, disbursement of new money to the consumer, or the rescheduling of payments under an existing obligation. Note that the finance charge on the new disclosure must include any unearned portion of the old finance charge that is not credited to the existing obligation.

Some transactions are not considered refinancings even if the transaction technically meets the definition of "refinancing," including:

- Renewal of an obligation with a single payment of principal and interest or

Truth in Lending Act

with periodic interest payments and a final payment of principal without a change in the original terms;

- An APR reduction with a corresponding change in the payment schedule; and

- Changes in credit terms arising from the consumer's default or delinquency (under some circumstances this type of transaction may be considered a refinancing).

Finance Charge Tolerances

In a refinancing of a residential mortgage transaction where no money is advanced and there is no consolidation of an existing loan, the finance charge is accurate if:

- It is understated by no more than 1 percent of the face amount of the note or $100, whichever is greater; or

- It is greater than the amount required to be disclosed.

> In a refinancing with no new money and no consolidation, an institution will have accurately disclosed the finance changes if the finance change disclosed is higher than the actual finance charge or if it is understated by no more than the higher of $100 or 1% or the face amount of the note.

Multiple Creditors or Consumers

If the credit transaction involves more than one creditor, the creditors must agree which one will comply with the disclosure requirements. A single, complete set of disclosures must be provided, rather than partial disclosures from several creditors.

If there is more than one consumer, the disclosures may be made to any consumer who is primarily liable on the obligation. The disclosures may not be made only to an endorser, guarantor, or similar party who is not primarily liable. For secured loans subject to rescission, one copy of material disclosures and two copies of the rescission notice must be given to each person who has the right to rescind the transaction.

Annual Percentage Rate (APR)

"Annual percentage rate" (APR) is a measure of the total cost of credit, expressed as a nominal yearly rate. It represents the total finance charge on a loan and relates the amount and timing of value received by the consumer to the amount and timing of payments made. APR includes costs such as transaction charges or premiums for credit guarantee insurance.

Since APR does not rely on state law definitions of interest, it is not an "interest" rate. It includes charges, such as a commitment fee paid by the consumer, not viewed by some state usury statutes as interest. Conversely, an APR might not include a charge, such as a credit report fee in a real property transaction, which some state laws might view as interest.

Disclosure of the APR is central to the uniform credit cost disclosure envisioned by TILA. Although use of add-on and discount rates in calculating interest still is permitted, it is not permissible to quote those rates, even if the APR is quoted with them. When quoting interest rates either orally or in written documents, the institution always must use the APR.

For details on calculating the APR see the appendices of Regulation Z. Appendix D covers construction loans, Appendix F covers open-end credit plans, and Appendix J covers closed-end credit plans.

APR Accuracy Tolerances

Regulation Z provides tolerances for APR accuracy for both open-end and closed-end credit. The disclosed APR on an open-end credit account is accurate if it is within one-eighth of 1 percent of the APR calculated under Regulation Z.

The disclosed APR on a closed-end transaction is accurate for:

- Regular transactions (any single advance transaction with an irregular first payment period and/or a first or last irregular payment), if it is within one-eighth of 1 percent of the APR calculated under Regulation Z; and

- Irregular transactions (such as multiple advances), if it is within one-fourth of 1 percent of the APR calculated under Regulation Z.

There are *additional* APR tolerances in mortgage transactions where the disclosed APR results from a finance charge that is incorrect but within the tolerance limits. Under this provision, if the disclosed APR varies from the actual rate, the disclosed APR will be considered accurate if:

- The rate results from the disclosed finance charge; and

- The disclosed finance charge would be considered accurate in a mortgage loan transaction (see Finance Charge Tolerances); or

- The disclosed finance charge would be considered accurate (within tolerance limitations) for rescission, refinancing, or foreclosure purposes. (See Refinancing, Right to Rescission, and Special Foreclosure Rules in this section.)

> There are *additional* APR tolerances in mortgage transactions where the disclosed APR results from a finance charge that is incorrect but within the tolerance limit.

Finance Charge

The Federal Reserve changed Regulation Z to establish new accuracy tolerances in finance charge disclosures. The agency also offered guidance on the charges a lender must normally include and exclude from the disclosed finance charge.

The "finance charge" is a measure of the cost of consumer credit expressed in dollars and cents. Regulation Z requires that the finance charge be disclosed to the consumer along with the APR. Finance charges include any charges or fees payable directly or indirectly by the consumer and imposed directly or indirectly by the financial institution either as an incident to or as a condition of an extension of consumer credit.

Bankers often encounter difficulties when using the 360- or 365-day year in computing interest. Regulation Z permits banks to disregard the fact that months have different numbers of days when calculating and making disclosures, even if a bank's practice is to take account of the variations in months to collect interest. Disclosure violations may occur, however, when a bank applies a daily interest factor based on a 360-day year to the actual number of days between payments. In those situations, the bank must disclose the higher values of the finance charge, the APR, and the payment schedule resulting from this practice.

Regulation Z contains no tolerance for inaccurate finance charge disclosures for open-end credit. However, Regulation Z does tolerate a limited inaccuracy in stating the finance charge for closed-end credit. The disclosed finance charge in a closed-end credit transaction for a *nonmortgage loan* is accurate if:

- It is not more than $5 above or below the exact finance charge and the transaction involves an amount financed of $1,000 or less; or

- It is not more than $10 above or below the exact finance charge and the transaction involves an amount financed of more than $1,000.

The amendments established new, greater tolerances in accuracy in disclosing the finance charge in connection with closed-end loans secured by real property or dwellings (*mortgage loans*). A disclosed finance charge for a mortgage loan is accurate if:

- It is understated by no more than $100; or

- It is greater than the amount required to be disclosed.

Different tolerances apply in determining whether the right of rescission remains open beyond the standard three-day rescission period.

Charges Included

Fees and charges normally required to be included in the disclosed finance charge are:

- Amounts charged by a third party (someone other than the creditor), if the creditor requires the use of a third party as a condition of or an incident to the extension of credit or retains a portion of the third-party charge;

- Fees charged by a third party that conducts the loan closing (such as a settlement agent, attorney, or title company) if the creditor requires the particular services, the imposition of the charge, or retains a portion of the third-party charge;

- Interest, add-on, or discount charges;

- Service, transaction, or carrying charges;

- Points (except seller's points), loan fees, assumption fees, finder's fees, and similar charges;

- Appraisal, investigation, and credit report fees (except for loans secured by real estate on a consumer's principal dwelling);

- Premiums for required credit life, accident, health, or loss-of-income insurance.

- Premiums for credit guarantee insurance;

- Charges imposed on a creditor for purchasing or accepting a consumer's obligation, if the consumer is required to pay the charges in cash, as an addition to the obligation or as a deduction from the proceeds of the obligation;

- Inspection fees for the staged disbursement of construction loan proceeds;

- Borrower-paid mortgage broker fees, in consumer credit transactions secured by real property or a dwelling, including fees paid directly to the broker or the lender for delivery to the broker. Such a fee may be excluded from the finance charge if the fee would be excluded when charged by the creditor;

- Discounts for the purpose of inducing payment by a means other than the use of credit;

- Charges or premiums paid for debt cancellation coverage written in connection with a credit transaction, whether or not the coverage is insurance under applicable law. This includes GAP (guaranteed automobile protection) agreements sold in connection with motor vehicle loans. A fee charge for voluntary debt cancellation may be excluded from the finance charge if certain conditions are met;

- Annuity premiums in connection with reverse mortgage transactions if the creditor requires the purchase of the annuity incident to the credit;

- Charges for a required maintenance or service contract imposed only in a credit transaction;

- Tax imposed by a state or other governmental body solely on a creditor, if the creditor separately imposes the charge on the consumer;

- Premiums for annuities offered in connection with a reverse mortgage transaction if the creditor requires the purchase of the annuity incident to the credit;

- Fees for preparing a Truth in Lending disclosure statement.

Charges Excluded

Fees and charges that are always excluded from the disclosed finance charge are:

- Charges imposed uniformly in cash and credit transactions, including taxes, license fees, registration fees, and quantity discounts;

- Discounts available to a particular group of consumers if they are members of certain organizations or have accounts at a particular financial institution;

- Charges for service policy, auto club membership, or policy of insurance against latent defects offered to or required of both cash and credit customers for the same price;

- Charges for actual unanticipated late payment, for exceeding a credit limit, or for delinquency, default, or a similar occurrence;

- Charges imposed by a financial institution for paying items that overdraw an account, unless the payment of such items and the imposition of the charge were previously agreed upon in writing;

- Application fees charged to all applicants for credit, whether or not credit is extended. Such fees may include the cost of appraisals, credit investigations, and credit reports;

- Charges that would be a finance charge if they were imposed on the consumer separately, but that are instead absorbed by the financial institution as a cost of doing business;

- Seller's points, which include any charges imposed by the creditor on a noncreditor seller for providing credit to the buyer or for providing credit on certain terms;

- Interest forfeited as a result of an interest reduction required by federal or state law on a time deposit used as security for an extension of credit;

- The following fees when reasonable and bona fide and imposed in connection with a loan secured by real estate or by the principal dwelling of a borrower or guarantor:

    - Fees for title examination or abstracting, title insurance, or property surveys;

    - Fees for preparing loan-related documents;

    - Notary, appraisal, inspection (including pest infestation and flood hazard inspections conducted prior to closing), and credit report fees;

- Amounts paid into escrow accounts for charges that are not themselves included in the disclosed finance charge (such as future water or sewer charges);

- Discounts offered to induce payment for a purchase by cash, check, or other means; and

- Certain security interest charges, if itemized, disclosed, and paid to public officials. Examples include: charges, or other fees required for filing or recording security instruments, mortgages, continuation statements, termination statements, and similar documents, as well as intangible property or other taxes.

Open-End Credit

Open-end credit plans such as credit card and overdraft checking accounts require two basic types of required disclosures: those made before the first transaction on the account, and those made on each periodic billing statement for transactions occurring during the period.

Issuance of Credit Cards

Financial institutions cannot issue unsolicited credit cards. They may issue a credit card only if it is requested or applied for, or if it is a renewal of, or in substitution for, an accepted credit card. Both written and oral requests are permissible. Financial institutions may respond to a request by issuing a card to the person making the request or to any authorized user for whom that person requests a card.

Financial institutions may issue a personal identification number (PIN) to an existing cardholder without a specific request from the consumer, provided that the PIN, by itself, cannot be used to obtain credit. When renewal or substitution occurs, each accepted card may be replaced by no more than one renewal or substitute card.

Application Disclosures

A creditor who invites a consumer to complete and submit an application must provide early disclosure with the application. The disclosures required vary depending on whether the application is solicited by direct mail, by telephone, or by other means available to the general public, such as catalogs or point-of-sale distribution. Early disclosures are not required for advertisements or other invitations to open an account that do not include an application.

Solicitation by mail of an application must include all of the early disclosures listed below. If the application is made by telephone, then disclosures 1 through 6 below must be made orally unless the card issuer does not impose a fee or the issuer does not impose a fee unless the consumer uses the card. Even then the issuer is still required to make the disclosures listed below within 30 days of the consumer's request (but before the card is delivered).

The required early disclosures are:

1. Annual percentage rate, including information about variable and introductory rates;

2. Fees for issuance or availability;

3. Minimum finance charge;

4. Transaction charges;

5. Grace period;

6. Balance computation method;

7. Statement on charge card payments;

8. Cash advance fee;

9. Late payment fee; and

10. Over-the-limit fee.

A creditor soliciting the public to submit credit card applications found in magazines, catalogs, or at points of sale has three options for early disclosures. One option is to use the same disclosures listed above for mail solicitations, setting forth an APR used within 30 days before the information was printed and providing a toll-free telephone number for current information. The other two options call for less complete disclosures.

Initial Disclosures

Under an open-end credit plan, the financial institution must deliver to the consumer an initial disclosure statement before the consumer becomes obligated. These disclosures must be given even when they duplicate early disclosures given in soliciting a credit card application. The required initial disclosures are:

- Conditions under which a finance charge begins to accrue, including any time period within which any credit extended may be paid without incurring a finance charge;

- Periodic rate and corresponding annual percentage rate, including conditions under which different rates may be imposed and information about any variable rates;

- Explanation of the method of determining the balance on which the finance charge is computed;

- Method of determining the finance charge;

- Amount of any charges other than finance charges (i.e., late payment charges) that may be imposed, or an explanation of the method of determining such other charges;

- Any security interest the institution will acquire in any property, including notice of rescission right if such property is a consumer's principal dwelling;

Truth in Lending Act

- Statement outlining the consumer's right to dispute billing errors, and the creditor's responsibilities in the error resolution process; and

- Home equity plan information.

Variable Rate Information

If an open-end credit plan uses a variable rate, the financial institution must disclose when the rate may increase, any limitations on the increase, and the effects of an increase.

Subsequent Disclosures

Financial institutions are required to send a copy of consumer's rights and the creditor's responsibilities to the cardholder at least once each year. As an alternative to providing the statement annually, institutions may send a summary statement to the consumer with each periodic statement. This statement does not need to be in a form that the consumer can keep.

Periodic Statement Disclosures

A financial institution must send the consumer a periodic statement at the end of each billing cycle if either the ending balance exceeded $1 or a finance charge was imposed during the period. Alternatively, consumers may pick up, call, or have their statement provided by electronic means. If the institution offers a free-ride period (i.e., a period during which the consumer may avoid finance charges by paying the full balance due), the institution forfeits any finance or other charges for the period if the periodic statement is not sent to the consumer 14 days before the due date.

Each periodic statement must disclose the following:

- Previous balance;

- Identification of each credit transaction;

- Account credits;

- Periodic rates and corresponding annual percentage rates applicable to the account during the period, even if such rates were not in fact imposed;

- Balance to which each periodic rate was applied and an explanation of how the finance charge balance was determined, including the amount of any credits or payments not deducted in computing the balance;

- Amount of the finance charge added or debited to the consumer's account during the billing cycle;

- Annual percentage rate when a finance charge is imposed during the billing cycle;

- Amount and itemization of any charges other than finance charges debited during the cycle;

- Closing date of the billing cycle and the account balance outstanding on that date;

- Free-ride period, including the date by which payment must be made to avoid finance charges; and

- Address for notice of billing errors.

Additional Disclosures

TILA requires that institutions send notification of the annual fee to the consumer at least 30 days before assessing the charge. Institutions also are required to notify the consumer by what date he/she must notify the institution that the consumer wishes to cancel the card without paying the annual fee.

In addition, institutions are required to send a notice to cardholders if the institution changes providers of credit card insurance. The notice should indicate any increase in the rate, any substantial decrease in the coverage, and a statement that the cardholder may discontinue the insurance.

Transaction Identification

Financial institutions must identify credit transactions on or with the first periodic statement reflecting the transaction. In the case of sale credit (purchases involving the use of a credit card, or some other means of accessing an open-end line of credit, to obtain goods or services from a merchant), the following rules apply to the identification required:

- If a copy of the actual document evidencing the purchase transaction is included, the enclosed copy or periodic statement must reflect the amount of the transaction and either the date of the transaction or the date the charge is debited to the consumer's account;

- If a copy of the credit document is not included with the statement, and if the creditor and seller are the same or related persons, the statement must reflect the transaction date and amount and a brief identification of the property or services purchased; and

- If a copy of the credit document is not provided, and if the creditor and seller are not the same or related persons, the statement must reflect the transaction date and amount, and the seller's name, city, and state where the transaction occurred.

In the case of nonsale credit (loan credit, such as advances and overdraft checking), the following disclosures are required:

- Identification of the transaction, or an actual copy of the receipt or credit document;

- Amount of the transaction; and

- At least one of the following dates: the transaction date, the debiting date, or, if the consumer signed the credit document, the date on the document.

Crediting Payments and Refunds

Payments must be credited as of the date of receipt, regardless of when they are posted, if failure to do so results in the imposition of a finance, late, or similar charge. If the financial institution fails to credit a payment promptly, and, as a result, a finance or other charge is imposed, the consumer's account must be credited in that amount during the next billing cycle. If a financial institution specifies on or with the periodic statement reasonable requirements for making payments, but it accepts payments that do not conform to the requirements, then it has five days from the date of receipt to credit the non-conforming payment.

Sellers of goods or services purchased with credit cards, and card-issuing financial institutions, must act within the following deadlines when the seller agrees to refund the purchase price by putting through a credit to the card account:

- The seller must transmit a credit voucher to the financial institution within seven business days from accepting the return (or forgiving a debt for services rendered); and

- The financial institution must credit the consumer's credit card account within three business days from receiving the credit voucher.

Cardholder Liability

A cardholder's maximum liability to the financial institution for unauthorized use of that card is the smaller of $50 or the cost of any goods or services purchased before the cardholder notified the institution of the card's loss, theft, or unauthorized use. Even this limited liability may be imposed only if:

- The credit card is an accepted one, that is, requested and actually received, or issued as a renewal or substitute and actually received;

- The financial institution has disclosed to the cardholder in writing the potential liability for unauthorized use of the card and the means of notifying the financial institution in case of loss or theft; and

- The financial institution has provided a means of identifying the cardholder or authorized user, such as a signature panel on the card.

If a financial institution tries to enforce liability for credit card use, it must show that the use was authorized or that the conditions for imposing the limited liability for unauthorized use have been met. If an institution issues 10 or more credit cards to employees of a firm for business use, the firm may agree to assume a greater liability for unauthorized use; but neither the institution nor the firm may impose on an employee any greater liability than permitted under TILA.

Prohibition of Offsets

A financial institution generally may not offset its consumer's credit card indebtedness against his or her deposit account, or place a hold on funds in the account. A customer may, however, specifically authorize a financial institution periodically to deduct all or a part of his or her credit card indebtedness from a deposit account. A financial institution also may collect a credit card indebtedness from a deposit account through any means generally available to other creditors, such as an attachment or other levy, enforcement of a court order or judgment, or by obtaining and enforcing a separate security interest to which the customer agreed and that was disclosed as required by Regulation Z.

Cardholder Claims and Defenses

A cardholder with a dispute about property or services purchased with a credit card may withhold payment from the institution under the following circumstances:

- The cardholder has made a good faith attempt to resolve the dispute with the merchant;

- The amount of the purchase exceeded $50; and

- The transaction occurred within the same state as the consumer's current designated address or within 100 miles of that address.

If the goods or services either were offered through a mail solicitation in which the institution participated, or sold by a party related to the institution, then the cardholder may withhold payment for a disputed purchase of any size at any location. If the above requirements are met, a financial institution may not report a consumer as delinquent until that dispute is settled or judgment has been rendered. The amount of the payment withheld is limited to the amount owing on the disputed transaction when the consumer first notifies the merchant or financial institution of the dispute. These dispute resolution procedures are inapplicable when the purchase is made with cash obtained through a credit card cash advance.

Billing Error Resolution

To allege a billing error, the consumer must notify the financial institution in writing of the alleged error. The notice must be received by the financial institution within 60 days after the periodic statement reflecting the alleged error was mailed or delivered to the consumer. The notice must contain sufficient information to:

- Identify the consumer's name and account number;

- Indicate the consumer's belief that an error occurred; and

- Describe the alleged error.

After receiving a billing error notice, the financial institution must acknowledge its receipt in writing to the consumer within 30 days. Within two billing cycles, but not more than 90 days after receipt of the billing error notice, the financial institution must either have corrected the billing error and sent the consumer an explanatory letter or corrected statement, or written to the consumer explaining why the financial institution believes the bill is correct.

The consumer may withhold payment on any portion of the required payment that the consumer believes is related to the disputed amount until the financial institution completes the resolution procedures. The financial institution must indicate on or with each periodic statement pending the resolution of the matter that the payment of any related finance or other charge is not required.

The financial institution is not allowed to make an adverse report to anyone on the consumer's credit standing, or report that the amount or account is delinquent, because the consumer has not paid the disputed amount and related finance or other charges. The financial institution may report that the amount or the account is in dispute.

Following the error resolution procedures, if the financial institution determines that the consumer owes all or part of the disputed amount and related finance or other charges, it must promptly notify the consumer in writing of the amount owed and when payment is due. Before the financial institution may report the amount or account as delinquent, the consumer must be given the benefit of any free-ride period listed in the initial disclosures, with a minimum of 10 days to pay the amount.

If the financial institution fails to follow any of the billing error resolution requirements, it may not collect the first $50 of a disputed amount, even if the bill is deemed correct.

Advertising Credit Terms

A financial institution may not use "bait" advertising, such as offering credit at a particular rate, unless it actually does or will offer or arrange credit on those terms. Also, no advertisement may set forth any of the required initial disclosures without also stating the following credit terms, as applicable:

- Any minimum, fixed, transaction, activity or similar charge that could be imposed;

- Any periodic rate that may be imposed, expressed as an APR;

- Whether the plan provides for a variable periodic rate; and

- Any membership fee that could be imposed.

Home Equity Lines of Credit

The 1988 TILA amendment changed the requirements for home equity lines of credit (HELCs). The changes affect HELC disclosures, advertising, and contract terms. Financial institutions must make HELC disclosures at least four times:

1. HELC disclosures and a brochure on or with the application;

2. Regular open-end initial disclosures, given before the first transaction;

3. A repeat of some of the HELC disclosures with the initial open-end disclosures; and

4. Periodic disclosures.

HELC Disclosures

An application for a HELC must be accompanied by the Federal Reserve Board's home equity brochure (or a suitable substitute) explaining operation of the HELC, and by the following disclosures:

- A direction to the consumer to retain the disclosures;

- The time for submitting the application to obtain the disclosed terms;

- Identification of terms subject to change before opening the HELC;

- A notice that all fees are refundable if the applicant elects not to enter the plan because of an intervening change in terms (other than the fluctuation in a variable-rate index);

- A description of the creditor's rights to close, limit, reduce, demand repayment, or alter the terms of the plan, and of the consumer's right to receive any nondisclosed conditions under which those rights would be exercised;

- A statement that the customer's dwelling secures the loan, and could be lost in event of default;

- Payment terms, including a $10,000 loan example showing the minimum periodic payment, any balloon payment, and the time it would take to repay the balance;

- Fees imposed by the creditor to open, use, or maintain the plan, and when such fees are payable;

- Fees imposed by a third party to open the plan; and

- The annual percentage rate.

HELC Variable Rates

If a HELC has a variable interest rate, then the institution must disclose:

- That the rate, payment, or term may change;

- That the APR excludes costs other than interest;

- The index or formula needed to make rate adjustments and the source;

- An explanation of how the rate will be determined;

- That the consumer should request the current index value, margin, discount or premium, and APR;

- That the initial rate is discounted, as applicable, and its duration;

- The frequency of APR changes;

- Rules on changes (ceilings and floors) to the index, APR, and payment amount, including information on payment limitations, negative amortization, and rate carryover;

- The lifetime rate cap for each payment option and whether there are any annual (or more frequent) caps, or a statement that there is no annual limitation;

- The minimum payment required for the draw and repayment periods and when the maximum rate may be imposed;

- A table based on a $10,000 extension of credit. The table must show how the APR and the minimum periodic payment amount would have been affected during the preceding 15 years by changes in the index used to compute the rate; and

- A statement that rate information will be provided on or with each periodic statement.

Truth in Lending Act

Restrictions on HELCs

HELC contract terms are limited as follows:

1. The variable rate index must be available publicly and not subject to the creditor's control;

2. The financial institution may terminate the HELC and demand immediate repayment only if:

   - The customer has committed fraud or a material misrepresentation;
   - The borrower fails to repay as agreed; or
   - The borrower has adversely affected the creditor's security;

3. The financial institution may reduce the credit limit or prohibit additional advances only during a period in which one of the following circumstances exists:

   - The value of the dwelling significantly declines;
   - The consumer's financial circumstances change materially;
   - The consumer defaults on a material obligation;
   - Government action restricts an APR increase;
   - Government action reduces the otherwise unencumbered equity to less than 120 percent of the HELC credit line;
   - A regulatory agency tells the financial institution that further advances would be unsafe or unsound; or
   - The maximum APR is reached;

4. The financial institution must notify the borrower of any reduced credit limit or restriction on further advances, informing the borrower if he or she must request reinstatement. If a request for reinstatement is not required, the financial institution must monitor the account to determine when conditions are reversed so that the original HELC limits are reinstated; and

5. Changes in the terms of a signed HELC contract are permissible only if:

   - The financial institution is permitted to terminate the HELC;

- The changes unequivocally benefit the consumer;

- The changes are insignificant;

- The change results from a specific event provided in the contract and does not otherwise contradict regulatory limitations;

- A new index is adopted because the old one becomes unavailable; or

- The consumer specifically agrees in writing to a change otherwise consistent with the regulation.

Closed-End Credit

Closed-end credit plans include direct installment loans by financial institutions, purchased dealer paper, single payment (time) loans, mortgage loans, demand loans, or any other credit arrangement that does not fall within the definition of open-end credit.

Disclosures

Financial institutions must furnish the required disclosures to a consumer before he or she becomes obligated contractually on the transaction. While this obligation usually arises when the consumer signs the note and receives the proceeds, it could arise sooner: for example, when the consumer accepts a loan commitment letter.

Disclosures must be clear, conspicuous, in writing, and presented in a way that does not obscure the relationship among the terms. Disclosures also must be in a form that the consumer can keep.

Certain required disclosures have to be grouped together, segregated from other material, and contain only information required to be disclosed or information directly related to required disclosures. Disclosures may be segregated from other material by appearing on a separate sheet of paper, being outlined in a box, or being set off by a different type style or color background.

In order to prevent consumer misunderstanding of important credit terms, the regulation requires that some closed-end credit information be identified using required terminology. Disclosures also must include a brief explanation of each of those terms. The required terms are "amount financed," "annual percentage rate," "finance charge," "total of payments," and "total sale price."

Required Disclosures

Financial institutions are required to disclose:

Creditor's Identity

The creditor's name must be disclosed. It may appear with or be made separately from the segregated disclosures. Disclosure of the creditor's address and telephone number is optional.

Amount Financed

The amount financed is the net amount of credit extended and is used to calculate the APR. A creditor must provide an itemization of the amount financed including: the amount of any proceeds distributed directly to the consumer, the amount credited to the consumer's account with the creditor, and any amounts paid to other persons by the creditor on the consumer's behalf.

Finance Charge

The finance charge is the measure of the cost of consumer credit as a dollar amount. The value of the finance charge must be disclosed as a single amount with the segregated disclosures, with the terms "finance charge" and "annual percentage rate" disclosed more conspicuously than other required disclosures. The elements of the finance charge may not be itemized in the segregated disclosures, although the regulation does not prohibit their itemization elsewhere.

Annual Percentage Rate

The annual percentage rate takes into account all relevant cost factors and provides a uniform measure of the cost of credit for comparing the cost of various credit plans. The value of the APR must be disclosed as a single rate only, whether the loan has a single interest rate, a variable interest rate, or graduated pay on separate interest rates, and it must appear with the segregated disclosures.

If the loan has a variable rate, the institution must make additional disclosures as to when or under what conditions the rate may change, any limitations on the increase, and the effects of an increase on the number or amount of payments.

The terms "finance charge" and "annual percentage rate" must be disclosed more conspicuously than other required disclosures.

Payment Schedule

The payment schedule disclosures must appear with the segregated disclosures and must state the number, amounts, and timing of payments scheduled to repay the obligation. The schedule must reflect all components of the finance charge, including, at a minimum, all payments scheduled to repay loan principal, and interest on the loan.

Total of Payments

Total of payments equals the sum of the payments included in the disclosed payment schedule or the sum of the amount financed and the finance charge (at the institution's option). This disclosure must appear with the segregated information.

Demand Feature Information

Disclosure of a demand feature is required on transactions that are payable on demand from the outset, as well as transactions that are not payable on demand at the time of consummation but convert to a demand status after a period. If the obligation has a demand feature, that fact must be disclosed with the segregated disclosures. If the obligation is payable on demand, disclosures must be based on an assumed maturity of one year.

Total Sale Price

If the seller is a creditor in the transaction, the transaction is a credit sale requiring disclosure of the total sale price, which is the sum of the cash price, the finance charge, and charges that are financed and not part of the finance charge. This disclosure is intended to allow a consumer to compare meaningfully the cost of buying on credit with a cash price purchase. The total sale price must appear with the segregated disclosures.

Prepayment Information

If a transaction provides for the payment of interest on the unpaid principal balance, a definitive statement must appear with the segregated disclosures indicating whether a penalty may be imposed if the obligation is prepaid in full.

If the transaction provides for a finance charge that does not take into account each scheduled reduction in the principal balance, a definitive statement must appear with the segregated disclosures indicating whether the consumer is entitled to a rebate of any finance charge if the obligation is paid in full.

If the transaction provides for the payment of interest on the unpaid principal balance but the amount of interest that will accrue over the loan term is less than the minimum finance charge, a statement must appear with the segregated disclosures indicating that the consumer is not entitled to a rebate of any finance charge if the obligation is prepaid in full.

Late Payment Information

Late payment information is required to appear with the segregated disclosures and should reflect accurately the predictable consequences of late payments. Only dollar or percentage charges that are incurred before maturity and added to individual delinquent installments need be disclosed.

Security Interest Information

A security interest is an interest in property that secures performance of a consumer credit obligation and is recognized by state or federal law. If the collateral securing the loan, whether owned by the consumer or a third party, is purchased as part of, or with the proceeds of, the credit transaction, the financial institution must briefly state that fact with the segregated disclosures.

In nonpurchase money transactions, any collateral securing the loan, whether owned by the consumer or a third party, must be identified briefly with the segregated disclosures by item or type.

Insurance Information and Debt Cancellation

If the financial institution elects to meet certain conditions, including making disclosures specified in the regulation, it may exclude from the finance charge any premiums for credit life, accident, health, or loss of income, insurance and any premiums for property or liability insurance, and debt cancellation fees. The insurance disclosures may, at the institution's option, appear either with the segregated disclosures or with any other information. If the insurance disclosures appear with the segregated disclosures, no additional explanatory material need be included.

With debt cancellation agreements, creditors may provide a disclosure that refers to debt cancellation coverage whether or not the coverage is considered insurance. Creditors may use the model credit insurance disclosures only if the debt cancellation coverage constitutes insurance under state law. Otherwise, they may provide a parallel disclosure that refers to debt cancellation coverage.

Security Interest Charges

If the financial institution elects to itemize and disclose fees set by law and payable to public officials for determining the existence of a security interest or for perfecting, releasing, or satisfying any security interest related to the credit transaction, or if it elects to itemize and disclose premiums payable for any insurance in lieu of perfecting a security interest, it may exclude such fees or premiums from the finance charge.

The security interest charges may, at the institution's option, appear either with the segregated disclosures or with any other information. Inclusion on a settlement statement required by the Real Estate Settlement Procedures Act satisfies the requirements.

A Reference to the Credit Contract

In addition to the other required disclosures, financial institutions must include a statement in the segregated disclosures that the consumer should refer to the appropriate contract document for information about nonpayment, default, the right to accelerate the maturity of the obligation, and prepayment rebates and penalties.

Assumption Policy Information

In a residential mortgage transaction, the financial institution must disclose, with the segregated disclosures, whether a subsequent purchaser of the dwelling may be permitted to assume the remaining obligation on its original terms. If the disclosure is an affirmative statement, it must reflect that the financial institution cannot determine, at the time of disclosure, whether a loan may be assumable on a future date on its original terms, if that is the case. The disclosure should not give any explanation of the criteria for conditions of assumability.

Required Deposit Information

If a financial institution requires the consumer to maintain a deposit as a condition of the specific transaction, it must disclose that the APR does not reflect the effect of that required deposit.

High-Rate/High-Fee Mortgages

Applicability

The Federal Reserve Board issued amendments to regulation Z implementing provisions of the Home Ownership and Equity Protection Act of 1994 dealing with certain mortgage loans bearing rates or fees above a certain percentage or amount, or high-rate/high-fee loans.

The high-rate/high-fee loan requirements of Regulation Z apply to consumer credit transactions secured by the consumer's principal dwelling, and in which either:

- The APR at consummation will exceed the yield on Treasury securities with a comparable maturity by more than 10 percentage points; or

- The total points or fees payable by the consumer at or before loan closing will exceed the greater of 8 percent of the total loan amount (the amount financed) or $412.

The requirements do not apply to:

- Residential mortgage transactions;

- Reverse mortgage transactions; or

- Open-ended credit plans.

Disclosures

A lender making a high-rate/high-fee mortgage loan will, in addition to the other TILA disclosures, be required to provide the following disclosure to the consumer:

> *You are not required to complete this agreement merely because you have received these disclosures or have signed a loan application. If you obtain this loan, the lender will have a mortgage on your home. You could lose your home, and any money you have put into it, if you do not meet your obligations under the loan.*

This disclosure must be made clearly and conspicuously and in a form that the consumer may keep. The disclosure must also disclose the APR on the loan, the amount of the regular payment on the loan and, if a variable rate loan, a statement that the interest rate and monthly payment may increase and the amount of the single maximum monthly payment that could apply to the loan.

The high-rate/high-fee disclosures must be made at least three business days prior to the consummation of the mortgage loan. If during the three days the creditor changes the terms of the loan making the disclosures inaccurate, new disclosures must be provided to the consumer. The new disclosures may be provided by telephone if the changes were initiated by the consumer, and if, at consummation, new written disclosures are provided and the consumer signs a statement that the new disclosures were provided by telephone at least three days before consummation of the loan.

The three-day waiting period may only be waived by the consumer in order to meet a bona fide financial emergency, such as avoiding foreclosure on the consumer's home. To modify, or waive, the three-day period, the consumer must provide the lender with a dated, written statement describing the emergency, specifically modifying or waiving the waiting period, and bearing the signatures of all of the consumers entitled to the waiting period.

Prohibited Terms for High-Rate/High-Fee Loans

A mortgage transaction subject to the high-rate/high-fee requirements of Regulation Z may not provide for the following terms:

- Balloon payments on loans with terms less than five years, except for bridge loans with a maturity of less than one year connected with the acquisition or construction of the consumer's principal dwelling;

- Negative amortization;

- Advance payments;

- Increased interest rate after default;

- Rebates, where the refund is calculated by a method less favorable than the actuarial method for rebates of interest arising from a loan acceleration due to default; or

- Prepayment penalties, unless: (1) the penalty can only be exercised for the first five years after consummation, (2) the source of the prepayment funds is not a refinancing by the creditor or an affiliate of the creditor, and (3) at consummation the consumer's debt to income ratio is 50 percent or less.

Prohibited Practices

A lender extending high-rate/high-fee mortgage loans may not:

- Engage in a pattern or practice of extending such credit to a consumer based on the consumer's collateral if the consumer's financial status indicates an inability to make the payments to repay the obligation;

- Pay a contractor under a home improvement contract from the proceeds of a high-rate/high-fee mortgage other than by an instrument payable to the contractor and consumer jointly or, at the election of the consumer, through a third-party escrow agent; or

- Sell or assign the mortgage without disclosing that it is subject to the high-rate/high-fee requirements of Regulation Z and that the purchasers or assignees could be liable for all claims and defenses with respect to the mortgage that the consumer could assert against the creditor.

Reverse Mortgages

The Federal Reserve Board issued amendments to Regulation Z implementing provisions of the Home Ownership and Equity Protection Act of 1994 dealing with reverse mortgage transactions.

A reverse mortgage transaction is a nonrecourse loan in which the consumer provides the lender with a security interest in the consumer's principal dwelling to secure one or more advances. The unique feature of reverse mortgage transactions is that any principal, interest, or shared appreciation or equity is due and payable only after the consumer dies, the dwelling is transferred, or the consumer ceases to occupy the dwelling as a principal dwelling. Reverse mortgages are primarily used by elderly homeowners who are relying on their home's value to generate additional cash flow.

Lenders must provide reverse mortgage borrowers with a notice stating that the consumer is not obligated to complete the reverse mortgage transaction merely because the consumer has received the required disclosures or has signed an application. The notice must be provided at least three business days prior to the consummation of a closed-end credit transaction or the first transaction under an open-end credit plan, and must also include:

- A good faith projection of the total cost of credit expressed as a table of "total annual loan cost rates";

- An itemization of pertinent loan terms, charges, the age of the youngest consumer, and the appraised property value; and

- An explanation of the "Total Annual Loan Cost Rate" table.

The table must show a minimum of nine total annual loan cost rates for no fewer than three projected appreciation rates and no fewer than three credit transaction periods. Regulation Z specifies that the three appreciation rates that must be used are 0 percent, 4 percent, and 8 percent. The three loan periods that must be used are two years, the actuarial life expectancy of the consumer obligated on the reverse mortgage, and 1.4 times the actual life expectancy of the consumer.

At the lender's option, a fourth loan period of one-half of the life expectancy may also be used. The Federal Reserve Board has included as Appendix K to Regulation Z a model reverse mortgage disclosure form, including a sample table, that can be used for these disclosures.

Right of Rescission

A consumer has the right to rescind a transaction if:

- A security interest is or will be acquired in the consumer's principal dwelling. A principal dwelling may be a boat, mobile home, or other property considered as personal under state law;

- The consumer has at least an ownership interest in the dwelling and that interest is encumbered by the financial institution's security interest;

- The security interest is retained as part of the credit transaction; and

- The transaction is subject to Regulation Z (right of rescission does not apply to business purpose credit).

The right of rescission does not apply to:

- A loan to acquire or construct the consumer's principal dwelling;

- A financing by the same financial institution of an extension of credit already secured by the consumer's principal dwelling; and

- A transaction in which a state agency is a creditor.

If a transaction is subject to the right of rescission, the consumer may cancel the transaction at any time before the end of the rescission period. The rescission period normally begins to run at the time a security interest is taken in the consumer's principal dwelling. It expires three complete business days after the latest of the following three events occurs:

1. Consummation of the transaction;

2. Delivery of all material disclosures: APR, finance charge, amount financed, total of payments, and payment schedule; or

3. Delivery of two copies of the required rescission notice to each consumer entitled to rescind the transaction.

If either the required notice or material disclosures are not delivered, or if the material disclosures are not within the applicable TILA tolerances, the rescission period continues to run until after the earliest of the following three events occurs:

1. Expiration of three years after the consummation of the transaction;

2. Transfer of all of the consumer's interest in the property; or

3. The sale of the property.

A creditor cannot be liable for the form of notice given to a consumer if the creditor used the appropriate form published by the Board or a comparable form.

Finance Charge Tolerances

A consumer does not have any extended rescission rights when finance charge disclosures are within the applicable tolerances. A finance charge, and any other disclosures affected by the finance charge, are to be within such tolerances if they are:

- Understated by no more than one-half of 1 percent of the face amount of the note or $100, whichever is greater; or

- Greater than the amount required to be disclosed.

Special Foreclosure Rules

After the initiation of a foreclosure on the consumer's principal dwelling, which secures a credit obligation, the consumer has the right to rescind the transaction if:

- An entire mortgage broker fee was not included in the finance charge (if required by the laws and regulations in effect at the time of consummation); or

- The creditor did not provide the appropriate form of notice.

After initiation of foreclosure, the finance charge is considered accurate if:

- It is understated by no more than $35; or

- It is greater than the amount required to be disclosed.

Violation Reimbursement

On July 11, 1980, the federal financial regulatory agencies issued a Joint Notice of Statement of Interagency Enforcement Policy for Truth in Lending ("policy guide"). The policy guide summarizes and explains the reimbursement provisions of the TILA. It also describes the corrective action that the financial regulatory agencies believe will be appropriate and generally intend to require when the TILA gives the agencies authority to order equitable remedial action. The regulatory agencies anticipate that most financial institutions will comply voluntarily with the reimbursement provisions of the TILA. However, if a financial institution does not act voluntarily to correct violations, the agencies are required by law to use their cease-and-desist authority to order correction.

Institution's Liability

Institutions may face civil and criminal liability as well as administrative enforcement actions for failing to comply with the TILA and its regulations. Willful noncompliance with any TILA requirement may result in fines up to $5,000 and/or imprisonment for up to one year. Civil liability may result in recovery by the consumer of actual damages, costs, and reasonable attorney's fees. Successful class actions may result in recoveries up to the lesser of $500,000 or 1 percent of the lender's net worth.

References

Laws:

12 U.S.C. 1601 et seq.

Regulations:

12 CFR Part 226 (Reg. Z) (FRB)

XXII. Truth in Savings Act

Introduction and Purpose 224

Covered Accounts 224

Account Disclosure 224

Distribution of Disclosures 227

Periodic Statements 229

Interest Payment 229

Advertising of Interest Rates and Terms of Accounts 230

Civil Liability 231

References 231

224 Consumer Banking Regulatory Handbook

Introduction and Purpose

The Truth in Savings Act ("TISA") and the Federal Reserve Board's implementing Regulation DD require clear and uniform disclosure of deposit account interest rates and fees so that customers may compare competing savings and investment options. The Act also imposes substantive contractual limitations on the method of calculating interest to assure that interest is paid on the full amount of principal for each calculation period.

Generally, TISA contains provisions governing:

- Calculation and posting of annual percentage yields (APY);

- Advertisements and solicitations;

- Account fee disclosures;

- Interest rate and compounding disclosures;

- Calculation of interest payments;

- Disclosure of interest and fees in periodic statements;

- Minimum deposit and balance deposits; and

- Administrative enforcement and civil liability.

Covered Accounts

Any domestic accounts that are held by or offered to consumers who are U.S. residents or resident aliens, including time, demand, savings, and NOW accounts, are covered by TISA and Regulation DD. TISA and Regulation DD do not cover accounts held by unincorporated nonbusiness associations of individuals.

Account Disclosure

TISA requires that each institution keep a detailed schedule of fees and charges, rates, and other terms and conditions applicable to each class of account. The schedule must be written in clear and plain language to help the consumer in understanding the terms of the accounts offered.

A financial institution must provide this schedule as an account disclosure to a consumer at the times and intervals discussed below.

Regulation DD requires that this disclosure include, with respect to interest rates:

- The APY and the interest rate, using those terms;

- For fixed rate accounts, the period during which any APY will be in effect; and

- For variable rate accounts:

    – A statement that the APY and interest rate may change;

    – How the interest rate is determined;

    – The frequency at which the APY may change; and

    – Any limitation on the amount that the interest rate may change.

With respect to compounding, balances, fees, and other terms, Regulation DD requires disclosure of the following:

- The frequency with which interest is compounded and credited;

- If consumers will forfeit interest if they close an account before the accrued interest is credited, a statement that interest will not be paid in such cases;

- Any minimum balance required to open an account, avoid the imposition of a fee, or obtain the disclosed APY;

- The method used to compute minimum balances and the balance on which interest will be earned — the same method must be used for both calculations;

- A statement of when interest begins to accrue on noncash deposits;

- A description of all fees and periodic service charges and penalties on accounts, and their amount, or an explanation on how they will be determined;

- Any limitations on the number or dollar amount of withdrawals or deposits; and

- The amount or type of any bonus, when the bonus will be provided, and any minimum balance and time requirement to obtain the bonus.

In addition, for time accounts (defined as an account with a maturity of at least seven days that is subject to an early withdrawal penalty of at least seven days' interest) Regulation DD also requires disclosure of:

- The maturity date;

- A statement that a penalty will or may be imposed for early withdrawal, how it is calculated, and the conditions for its assessment;

- If compounding occurs during the term and interest may be withdrawn prior to maturity, a statement that the annual percentage yield assumes that interest remains on deposit until maturity and that withdrawal will reduce earnings;

- A statement of whether the account will renew automatically at maturity;

- If the account renews automatically, a statement of whether the bank provides a grace period after renewal for withdrawal without penalty; and

- If the account will not renew automatically, a statement of whether interest will be paid after maturity if the consumer does not renew.

The Federal Reserve Board has under review a number of proposals that would require a more precise calculation of the APY for certain accounts. The goal is to structure a uniform method to give consumers an enhanced basis for effective comparison shopping. One proposal recommended clarifying and regulating crediting and compounding practices. Another planned to factor into the APY the frequency of interest payments. Underlying these proposals is the desire to redesign the APY to reflect the effect of compounding, as well as the time value of money when interest payments occur prior to maturity. In addressing related concerns, the Board adopted an interim rule, which will remain in effect until the Board issues its final decision on APY calculations.

Interim Rule Amending Regulation DD (TISA)

As of January 1995, depository institutions may disclose an APY equal to the contract interest rate for certain noncompounding multiyear CDs.

The rule only allows this disclosure for time accounts:

- With maturities greater than one year;

- That do not compound; but

- Require interest distributions at least annually.

The rule does not allow this disclosure for:

- Accounts that prohibit withdrawal of interest; or

- Accounts that permit (but do not require) interest distributions before maturity.

All institutions choosing to comply with this rule must include a brief narrative in their account disclosures and advertisements. The Federal Reserve Board has developed the following model narrative:

This account requires the distribution of interest and does not allow interest to remain in the account.

Currently, Congress is considering legislation that would repeal several provisions of TISA, including those calling for an APY. The Board has deferred action on the APY proposals, pending Congress's resolution of the legislative proposals. Accordingly, the 1995 interim rule shall remain in effect until the Board issues a final rule.

Distribution of Disclosures

Regulation DD mandates that the disclosures discussed above be provided to customers and potential customers at various times and intervals.

New Accounts

Depository institutions must provide account disclosures to consumers when an account is opened or a service is provided, whichever is earlier. An institution is deemed to have provided a service when it assesses a fee that is required to be disclosed. If the consumer is not physically present at the time an initial deposit is accepted, the schedule should be mailed to the depositor no later than 10 days after the date of initial deposit.

Regulation DD requires new account disclosures whenever:

- A consumer renews a CD that does not roll over automatically;

- A consumer renews a CD and changes *any* account term;

- An institution transfers funds from an account to open a new account not at the consumer's request, unless disclosures for both accounts (including any change-in-term notices) have previously been given (e.g., funds transferred in a MMDA to a NOW account because the customer exceeded the MMDA transaction limits); or

- An institution accepts deposits to an account that it considers closed for the purpose of treating accrued, but uncredited, interest as forfeited by the consumer.

New account disclosures are not required when the accounts are obtained by an institution through an acquisition of, or a merger with, another institution.

Upon Request

Depository institutions must provide account disclosures whenever a consumer requests one. If the consumer is not present at the institution when the request is made, the institution must mail or deliver the disclosure within a reasonable time. The Federal Reserve considers 10 business days a reasonable time. Account disclosure is required when a consumer *requests* written information about an account, but is not required when there is merely an *oral inquiry* as to rates and yields or fees.

This disclosure may include the interest rate and APY offered within the seven calendar days preceding the date that the disclosure is sent. If these rates are used, the disclosure must state that they are accurate as of an identified date, and provide a telephone number consumers may call to obtain current rate information. In addition, the disclosure should state the maturity of a time account as a term rather than a date.

Change in Terms

Depositors must be notified of any adverse change to a term that is required to be disclosed. This notification must include a description of the change and its effective date. The disclosure must be mailed to depositors at least 30 days before the change takes effect. A single notification made to one of the holders of a multiple account is sufficient. No notification is required for interest rate changes on variable-rate accounts, changes in check printing fees, and changes in any term for accounts with maturities of one month or less.

When a new regulation is published affecting an account for which statements are delivered on a quarterly or more frequent basis, the institution must notify affected depositors that they have the right to request an updated account schedule. The notification must be mailed within 180 days after publication of the regulation.

Time Account Maturities

In the case of any time deposits with maturities greater than one month that are renewable at maturity without notice from the depositor, the disclosure must be mailed or delivered at least 30 calendar days before the date of maturity. Alternatively, disclosures may be mailed or delivered at least 20 calendar days before the end of the grace period, provided that the grace period is at least five days long. The following additional provisions apply:

- For time deposits with maturities of one year or less, but longer than one month, an institution must *either* (1) make a full disclosure, or (2) disclose only the terms that have changed since the prior disclosure.

- For time deposits with maturities of one month or less that renew automatically, an institution must disclose the terms that have changed since the prior disclosure, other than changes in interest rates.

- For time deposits with maturities of greater than one year that do not renew automatically, an institution need only disclose (1) the maturity date, and (2) whether interest will be paid after maturity. This disclosure must be made at least 10 calendar days before maturity.

Periodic Statements

Periodic statements given to each account holder must include clear and conspicuous disclosure of the following:

- Annual percentage yield earned;

- Amount of interest earned;

- Amount of any fees or charges imposed; and

- Number of days in the reporting period.

Financial institutions should sample and review periodic statements to assure that they are consistent with initial account-opening disclosures.

Interest Payment

Interest must be calculated on the full amount of principal in the account for each day of the stated calculation period by either the daily balance or average daily balance methods. Institutions must use the same balance calculation method when determining minimum balance requirements. Neither TISA nor Regulation DD mandates any particular interest-compounding period or frequency.

Interest must begin to accrue no later than the business day on which the funds are provisionally credited under the Expedited Funds Availability Act and Federal Reserve Board Regulation CC. TISA thereby prohibits use of the "ending balance" method (paying interest on the balance at the end of the period), the "investable balance" method (paying interest on balances less reserve requirements), and the "low balance" method (paying interest on the lowest daily balance as if it were the average daily balance).

Advertising of Interest Rates and Terms of Accounts

TISA mandates certain disclosure requirements for advertisements, announcements, or other solicitations for deposit accounts. Advertisements may not be misleading, inaccurate, or misrepresent a deposit contract. Advertisements may not refer to or describe an account as "free" or "no cost" (or a similar term) if any maintenance or activity fee may be imposed on the account. In addition, the word "profit" may not be used in referring to the interest paid on an account.

When an institution refers to interest payable, yields, or rates of interest on demand or interest-bearing accounts, it must also include clear, conspicuous, and proximate disclosure of:

- The APY;

- Whether rates are variable and how and when they may change;

- The period during which the APY will be offered, or a statement that it is accurate as of a specified date;

- Any minimum account balance;

- Any time requirements that must be met to earn the advertised yield;

- Any minimum amount of initial deposit in order to obtain that yield if the amount is greater than the minimum balance;

- Any transaction limits that apply to the account;

- A statement that regular fees or other conditions could reduce the yield;

- For time accounts, the term of the account and a statement that a penalty may be imposed for early withdrawal;

- A statement saying that an interest penalty is required for early withdrawal; and

- Any renewal policies and conditions.

If an advertisement refers to a bonus, the advertisement must state:

- The time requirement to obtain the bonus;

- The minimum balance to obtain the bonus;

- The minimum balance to open the account if it is greater than the minimum necessary to obtain the bonus; and

- When the bonus will be provided.

Regulation DD requires fewer disclosures in broadcast messages, outdoor media, and telephone response machines. Such media only need disclose minimum balance requirements, the term of the account, and any requirements necessary to receive an advertised bonus. Certain lobby signs only need include the APY and a statement advising consumers to ask employees about applicable fees and terms.

Civil Liability

TISA creates civil liability for failure to comply with the Act and implementing regulations. Courts are required to award (1) the actual damages sustained by the plaintiff, and (2) an additional amount between $100 and $1,000. In the case of a class action suit, courts are required to award actual damages. Courts in a class action suit have discretion to award reasonable attorneys' fees, and additional damages up to the lesser of $500,000 and 1 percent of the net worth of the institution.

Likewise, institutions are required to retain evidence of compliance with TISA and Regulation DD for two years. An institution's primary supervisory agency may impose a longer record retention period to carry out its enforcement obligations.

References

Laws:

12 U.S.C. 4301 et seq.

Regulations:

12 CFR Part 230

Index

A

Abusive behavior, prohibited by debt collectors, 132–33
Access devices, for electronic fund transfer, 80–81
Adjustable rate mortgage rules
    adjustment notices, 10
    adjustment requirements, 9–10
    disclosure information, 8–9
    introduction and purpose, 8
    laws and regulations references, 10
    maximum interest rates, 10
    rate formula or index, 10
    special information booklet, 8
Adjustment notices, 10
Adverse action, 100
Adverse changes, notification of, 228
Advertising
    credit terms, 208
    deposit insurance, 77
    equal credit opportunity, 93
    interest on deposits, 167
    leasing, 62
    nondiscriminatory, 137
    Truth in Savings Act (TISA), 230–31
Affiliated business arrangements, 178–79
Age
    and ECOA application processing/evaluation, 95–96
    request for information of, 139
Age Discrimination in Employment Act of 1967, 107
Agreement Corporations, Edge Act and, 154
Aliens, TIN not required for, 41–42
Alimony, request for information of, 94
American Exchange's Emerging Company Marketplace, 21
American Stock Exchange, 22–23
Annual fees, disclosure of, 204
Annual percentage rate (APR), 194, 195–96, 212, 213–14
Annual percentage rate (APR) accuracy tolerances, 196–97
Annual percentage yields (APY), 224, 225, 226–27, 230
Annunzio-Wylie Anti-Money Laundering Act of 1992, 19
Antidiscrimination Rule, 91–92
Application disclosures, 201–2
Applications, nondiscrimination in, 138
Appraisals, 97–98
    nondiscrimination in, 138
Assumption without lender approval, 171
ATM. *See* Automated teller machines (ATM)
Attorney General, 103
Automated teller machines (ATM)
    deposit-taking, 46
    exceptions to funds transfer rules, 35
    and notice of fund availability, 119–20

B

Bank, definition of, 21
Bank Enterprise Act (BEA) of 1991
    banking in distressed communities, 13–14
    community development financial institutions fund, 14–16
    introduction and purpose, 12
    laws and regulations references, 16
    lifeline accounts, 12
Bank Enterprise Awards Program, 14, 15–16
Bank Insurance Fund (BIF), 72
Bank Secrecy Act (BSA) of 1970
    amendment to, 4, 21
    compliance program, 39–40
    currency transaction report (CTR), 19–20
    currency transaction report (CTR) exemptions, 21–26
    foreign bank account reporting (FBAR), 39
    forfeiture, 37
    funds transfers, 31–35
    institutions subject to, 19
    introduction and purpose, 19
    "know your customer" requirements, 35–36, 37
    laws, regulations, and agency guidelines references, 43–44
    monetary instruments transaction records, 27–28
    other record-keeping requirements, 40–43
    payable through accounts (PTA), 28–29
    registration of nondepository institutions, 43
    structuring of transactions, 30–31
    suspicious transactions, 30
    transportation of currency and monetary instruments (CMIR), 37–38
Banking day, 112, 120
Beneficiary, in funds transfers, 31
Beneficiary's institution, 32
    payment order information (travel rule), 34
Branch-closing notice, 54–55
Brokered deposits, 75
Brokers' fees, 167

Business credit, 103
    and signature requirements, 99
Business day, 112
Business loans, 55, 171

C

Certificate of deposit (CD), 226, 227
Check kiting, 116
Checking accounts
    demand deposit, 166–67
    lifeline, 12
    See also Expedited Funds Availability Act
Checks, deposit of and fund availability. *See* Expedited Funds Availability Act
Child support, request for information of, 94
Childbearing
    and ECOA application processing/evaluation, 96
    request for information of, 94–95
CHIPS system, 34
Citizenship, and ECOA application processing/evaluation, 96–97
Civil liability, Truth in Savings Act (TISA), 231
Civil Rights Act of 1964, Title VII of the, 106–07
Civil Rights Act of 1968, Title VIII of the, 146
Closed-end credit
    definition of, 193, 212
    disclosures. *See* Closed-end credit disclosures
    high-rate/high fee mortgages, 217–19
    institution's liability, 222
    mortgages, 219–20
    right of rescission, 220–22
    special foreclosure rules, 221–22
    violation reimbursement, 222
Closed-end credit disclosures, 212
    amount financed, 212, 213
    annual percentage rate (APR), 196, 212, 213–14
    assumption policy information, 216
    creditor's identity, 213
    demand feature information, 214
    finance charge, 197, 212, 213, 221
    high-rate/high fee mortgages, 217–18
    insurance information and debt cancellation, 215–16
    late payment information, 215
    payment schedule, 214
    prepayment information, 214–15
    reference to the credit contract, 216
    required deposit information, 216
    security interest charges, 216
    security interest information, 215
    total of payments, 212, 214
    total sale price, 212, 214
Closing statements, 174
Comaker, 125
Commercial Banking Regulatory Handbook, The, 3
Commodity Futures Trading Commission, 193
Common carrier exemptions (CMFR), 38
Community Development Financial Institutions Act of 1994, 14
Community Development Financial Institutions Fund, 14–16

Community Development Financial Institutions Program, 14, 15
Community development loans, 56
Community development organization, 14
Community development test, 50, 52–53, 55
Community Enterprise Assessment Credit Board, 13
Community Reinvestment Act (CRA)
    assessment area, 46, 48, 49, 56
    branch-closing notice, 54–55
    community development test, 50, 52–53, 55
    data collection, reporting and disclosure, 46, 55–56, 155
    disclosure statement, 49
    fair lending examinations, 138
    introduction and purpose, 46
    laws and regulations references, 56
    lending, investment, and service tests, 50–52, 55
    performance evaluations, 46, 48, 49–50
    public file maintenance, 46, 48–49
    public notice of, 47–48
    small-institution performance standards, 50, 53, 55
    statement documenting programs, 46, 47–48
    strategic-plan evaluation, 50, 53–54, 55
Compliance examination, 4–5
Compliance Link, The, 3
Compliance program, BSA, 39–40
Computer software & systems, aggregate multiple transactions, 21
"Confession of judgment," 66, 67
Consumer
    definition of, 66
    protection. *See* Right to Financial Privacy Act
Consumer Banking Regulatory Handbook, The, 3
Consumer Credit Protection Act, 91, 191
Consumer Handbook on Adjustable Rate Mortgages, 8
Consumer Leasing Act
    advertising of lease, 62
    disclosures, 58–62
    introduction and purpose, 58
    laws and regulations references, 63
    leases covered and not covered, 58
    penalties and liabilities, 63
    record retention, 62
    relation to state law, 62–63
    renegotiations and extensions, 62
Consumer reports and reporting agencies. *See* Fair Credit Reporting Act
Corporate "know your customer," 36
Corporations, as exempt entities, 22–23
Cosigner, 68–69
    signature requirements, 99
Cranston-Gonzalez National Affordable Housing Act, 182
Credit. *See* Equal Credit Opportunity Act
Credit cards. *See* Truth in Lending Act (TILA)
Credit history
    and ECOA application processing/evaluation, 96–97
    and signature requirements, 99
Credit Practice Rules
    "cosigner" definition of, 68–69
    "earnings" definition of, 67
    "household goods" definition of, 67

Credit Practice Rules *(continued)*
    introduction and purpose, 66
    laws and regulations references, 69
    permitted contract provisions, 66–67
    prohibited contract provisions, 66
    prohibited practices, 68
    transactions covered, 66
Credit reports and reporting agencies. *See* Fair Credit Reporting Act
Credit scoring system, 95
Criminal activity, forfeiture and, 37
Criminal Code, 37, 184
Currency and monetary instruments (CMIR), transport of, 37–38
Currency transaction report (CTR), 22
    aggregation of multiple, 21
    exemptions. *See* Currency transaction report (CTR) exemptions
    filing of, 19, 20, 22
    information required, 20
Currency transaction report (CTR) exemptions, 21–22
    customer exemption statement, 25–26
    determination of an exempt entity, 22–23
    exempt customer list, 26
    general exemptions, 24
    limitations of exemptions, 23
    limited safe harbor, 23
    revocation of exemption, 24
    special exemptions, 24, 25
    unilateral exemptions, 24–25
Customer
    definition of, 186
    protection. *See* Right to Financial Privacy Act
Customs Service, 37, 38

D

Dealer, 172
Dealer loans, 172
Debt collection. *See* Fair Debt Collection Practices Act
Delinquency charges, disclosure of (CLA), 60
Demand deposit accounts, 112, 166–67
Demographic information
    Equal Credit Opportunity Act and, 93–95
    Fair Housing Act and, 139–40
Department of Justice (DOJ), 93, 136
Department of Labor, 106, 108, 109
Department of Veterans Affairs, 161
Deposit account records, 76
Deposit account requirements, 164–66
Deposit insurance
    advertisements of, 77
    categories of ownership, 73–74
    deposits held on another's behalf, 76
    determining legal ownership, 76
    insured deposits, 72
    introduction and purpose, 72
    laws and regulations references, 77
    limit of, 72–73
    official signs requirements, 76–77

Deposit insurance *(continued)*
    pass-through insurance, 74–76
Deposit insurance assessment credit, 14
Deposit slips, and notice of fund availability, 119
Depository Institutions Deregulation and Monetary Control Act of 1980, 164
Depository Institutions Deregulation Committee (DIDC), 164
Deposits, and availability of funds. *See* Expedited Funds Availability Act
Deposits, interest on. *See* Interest on deposits
"Designation of Exempt Person," 22
Disclosure statement, ARM, 8–9
Discrimination. *See* Equal Credit Opportunity Act (ECOA); Equal Employment Opportunity Act; Fair Housing Act
Disparate impact, 92–93
Disparate treatment, 92
Distressed communities, 13–14
Dwelling, definition of, 136, 155

E

Early termination, disclosure of (CLA), 60
Earnings
    assignment of, 66, 67
    definition of, 67
"Edgar," 23
Edge Act and Agreement Corporations, 154
Electronic fund transfer (EFT), 80
Electronic Fund Transfer Act (EFTA) of 1978, 35
    consumer liability, 86–87
    disclosures, 81–84
    error resolution procedures, 84–86
    introduction and purpose, 80
    issuance of access devices, 80–81
    laws and regulations references, 88
    notification of unauthorized transfer, 87–88
    transactions covered and not covered, 80
Emergency conditions, and funds availability, 116–17
Employee training, Expedited Funds Availability Act and, 121
Employer-employee referral fee exemption, 177–78
Employment
    denial of based on a consumer report, 127
    See also Equal Employment Opportunity Act
"Ending balance" method, 229
Entities, determination of exempt, 22–23
Entities exercising governmental authority, 21
Equal Credit Opportunity Act (ECOA)
    advertising, 93
    agency referrals, 103
    application processing and evaluation, 95–97, 100–101
    applications and information gathering, 93–95
    appraisals, 97–98
    business credit exceptions, 103
    corrective action, 104
    credit extension, 98–100
    furnishing credit information, 101
    general antidiscrimination rule, 91–92
    government monitoring information, 102
    indirect lending disclosure, 102

Equal Credit Opportunity Act (ECOA) *(continued)*
    introduction and purpose, 91
    laws and regulations references, 104
    loans covered by, 91
    notification, 100–101
    penalties, 104
    prequalification and preapproval programs, 101
    record retention, 102
    types of lending discrimination, 92–93
Equal Credit Opportunity Act (ECOA), fair lending examinations, 138
Equal Employment Opportunity Act
    Age Discrimination in Employment Act of 1967, 107
    agency guidance, 106
    Equal Pay Act of 1963, 107–8
    Executive Orders No. 11141 & No. 11246, 108–09
    introduction and purpose, 106
    laws and regulations references, 109–10
    Rehabilitation Act of 1973, 109
    summary of laws and regulations, 106
    Title VII of the Civil Rights Act of 1964, 106–07
    Vietnam Era Veterans Readjustment Act of 1974, 109
Equal Employment Opportunity Commission (EEOC), 106
"Equal Housing Lender" logo & poster, 137, 139
Equal Pay Act of 1963, 107–08
Error resolution procedures
    credit card billing, 207–08
    electronic fund transfers, 84–86
    Real Estate Settlement Procedures Act, 181
Escrow accounts, 175–76
    of flood insurance payments, 149
Escrow statements, 176–77
Executive Orders No. 11141 & No. 11246, 108–09
Exempt entities, determination of, 22–23
Expedited Funds Availability Act
    amendment to, 4
    availability of exception deposits, 118
    check collection, 121
    covered accounts, 112
    disclosures, 118–20
    employee training, 121
    exception notice, 117–18
    interest payments, 229
    introduction and purpose, 112
    laws and regulations references, 121
    local and nonlocal checks, 114
    next-day availability, 113
    $100 rule, 113–14
    overdrafts, 115
    payment of interest, 118
    reasonable cause to doubt collectibility, 115–17
    record retention, 120–21
    redeposited checks, 115
    safeguard exceptions, 114–17
    when funds are considered deposited, 120

F

Fair Credit Reporting Act (FCRA)
    consumer reporting agencies, 124, 125–26

Fair Credit Reporting Act (FCRA) *(continued)*
    coverage, 124
    denial of employment, 127
    disclosures, 124–25
    introduction and purpose, 124
    laws and regulations references, 127
    penalties and liabilities, 127
    prescreening, 126–27
    transactions not covered, 124
Fair Debt Collection Practices Act
    activities covered and not covered, 130
    communications with consumers, 130–31
    communications with third parties, 131–32
    deceptive forms, 134
    introduction and purpose, 130
    legal actions by debt collectors, 134
    legal reference, 134
    multiple debts, 134
    prohibited practices, 132–34
    validation of debts, 132
Fair Housing Act
    activities covered, 136
    equal housing lender logo & poster, 137, 139
    Fair Housing Home Loan Data System, 140–41
    fair lending examinations, 138–39
    introduction and purpose, 136
    laws and regulations references, 141
    loan application register reporting, 140
    monitoring information, 139–40
    prohibited discriminatory practices, 136–38
Fair Housing Home Loan Data System (FHHLDS), 140–41
Fair lending examinations, 138–39
Fair Lending Guidance: Responsibilities and Timeframes, 139
Farm loans, small, 55
Farmers Home Administration (FmHA), 155
Federal Deposit Insurance Corporation (FDIC), 12
Federal Deposit Insurance Corporation Improvement Act (FDICIA) of 1991, 54
Federal Emergency Management Agency (FEMA), 144, 146, 148, 149, 150
Federal Financial Institutions Examination Council (FFIEC), 154, 157
Federal Home Loan Bank, 24, 113, 118
Federal Home Loan Mortgage Corporation (FHLMC), 155
Federal Housing Administration (FHA), 155, 161
    loan prepayment disclosures, 182
    mortgage, 182
Federal Housing Authority, 145
Federal National Mortgage Association (FNMA), 155
Federal Reserve Banks, 24, 113, 118
Federal Reserve Board (FRB), 12
    credit practices, 66
    equal credit opportunity, 91
    finance charge tolerances, 197
    home equity brochure, 209
    home mortgage disclosure, 154
    Home Ownership and Equity Protection Act of 1994, 217, 219
    interest on deposits, 164

Federal Reserve Board (FRB), *(continued)*
    model reverse mortgage disclosure form, 220
    real estate settlement procedures, 173
    right to financial privacy, 187
    truth in savings, 224, 226–27, 228, 229
    See also under Regulations B through Z
Federal Rules of Civil or Criminal Procedure, 185
Federal Trade Commission (FTC), 66
Federal Trade Commission Act, 66
Fedwire, 80
    payment order information and, 33–34
Fee mortgages, high-rate/high, 217–19
Fees
    annual percentage rate (APR), 195–96
    disclosure of, 61, 197–99, 204
    finders' and brokers, 167
    referral, and kickbacks, 177–78
    for required statements, 179
FHA. *See* Federal Housing Administration (FHA)
Final rule exemptions, 21
Finance charge, 193, 194, 196, 197–200
Finance charge tolerances, 195, 197, 221
Financial Crimes Enforcement Network ("Fin CEN"), 22, 24
Financial institution responsibilities, 38
Financial privacy. *See* Right to Financial Privacy Act (RFPA)
Fixed-term (certificate) account, 164–65
Flood Disaster Protection Act of 1973 (FDPA)
    community requirements, 147
    insurance coverage, 147
    introduction and purpose, 144
    laws and regulations references, 151
    loans covered, 145–46
    mandatory flood insurance, 145
    mortgage portfolio protection plan (MPPP), 149–50
    National Flood Insurance Programs (NFIP), 144–45, 146, 147
    notification requirements, 147–49
    penalties, 150–52
    record-keeping requirements, 150–51
    regulatory requirements, 145
Flood Hazard and Boundary Maps, 144
Flood Insurance Rate Maps, 144
Foreclosure rules, 221–22
Foreign bank account reporting (FBAR), 39
Foreign bank accounts, 28
Foreign banks, and payment orders, 31–32
Foreign financial institutions, 38
Forfeiture law, Bank Secrecy Act and, 37
Form 851, 23
Form 4790, 37
Form 81-93, 146
Form 10-K, 23
Form TDF 90-22.1, 39
Forward-collection test, 121
457 Plan, 74
Free-ride period, 203
Funds transfer rules
    exceptions to, 35
    information retrieval and, 34–35
    international, 32

Funds transfer rules *(continued)*
    overview of, 31
    parties involved in, 31–32
    payment orders and, 31, 33–35
    record-keeping requirements, 32, 34

G

Garnishment, credit practice rules and, 67
Gender, request for information of, 94, 139
General Accounting Office (GAO), 185
Gifts to minors, deposit insurance coverage for, 74
Good faith estimate of settlement costs, 173–74
Governmental entities, exempt, 22
Guarantees, disclosure of (CLA), 60
Guarantor, 125

H

Harassment, prohibited by debt collectors, 132–33
High-rate/high fee mortgages, 217–19
Home equity lines of credit (HELCs), 156, 172, 209–12
    disclosures, 209–10
Home equity loans, 174
Home Mortgage Disclosure Act (HMDA)
    amendment to, 4
    data accuracy, 156
    data reporting under Community Reinvestment Act, 46, 55–56, 155
    disclosure statement, 49, 56, 157
    Fair Housing Act and, 138, 140–41
    home equity lines of credit, 156
    home mortgage loans, 56
    introduction and purpose, 154
    laws and regulations references, 157
    Loan/Application Register, 141, 156
    loans covered and excluded, 155
    nondepository mortgage lenders, 154
    public notice, 157
    submission of register, 157
Home Ownership and Equity Protection Act of 1994, 217, 219
Home-ownership counseling, 160–61
"Household goods," definition of, 67
Housing and Urban Development (HUD). *See* U.S. Department of Housing and Urban Development (HUD)
HUD. *See* U.S. Department of Housing and Urban Development (HUD)

I

Identification
    creditor's, 213
    of person receiving benefits, 179
    personal identification number (PIN), 201
    taxpayer identification number (TIN), 41–42
    transaction, 204–05
Income, and ECOA application processing/evaluation, 96
Individual ownership accounts, 73
Individual retirement accounts (IRAs), 74, 165

Insurance
    ECOA and, 99–100
    See also Deposit insurance; Flood Disaster Protection Act of 1973 (FDPA)
Insurance payments, 60
Insured deposits. See Deposit insurance
Interest on deposits, 118
    advertising, 167
    deposit account requirements, 164–66
    finders' and brokers' fees, 167
    introduction and purpose, 164
    laws and regulations references, 167–68
    premiums, 166–67
Interest payment, Truth in Savings Act (TISA), 229
Interest rate adjustments, 9
Interest rate changes (ARM), notice of, 10
Intermediary institutions, 32
    payment order information (travel rule), 34
Internal Revenue Code, 166, 185
Internal Revenue Service
    Affiliation Schedule (Form 851), 23
    Data Center, 20
    Model Customer Exemption Statement, 25
Internal transfers, 31
International Organization Immunities Act of Dec. 29, 1945 (22 U.S.C. 288), 41
"Investable balance" method, 229
Investment area, 15
Investment test, 51, 55
IRS. See Internal Revenue Service

J

Joint accounts, deposit insurance coverage for, 73–74
Joint applicants
    notification of credit, 101
    and signature requirements, 99
Joint credit, and marital status, 96
Joint Notice of Statement Interagency Enforcement Policy for Truth in Lending ("policy guide"), 222

K

Keoghs, 74, 165
Kickbacks, 177–78
"Know your customer" requirements, 35–36, 37

L

Land. See Property
Leases. See Consumer Leasing Act
Lending discrimination, types of, 92–93
Lending examinations, fair, 138–39
Lending test, 50–52, 55
Liability, disclosure of (CLA), 60–61
Lifeline account, 12
Limited purpose institutions, community development test, 52–53
Listed corporations, 21–22

Loan application register reporting, 140
Loan/Application Registers, 141, 156–57
Loan balance adjustments, 9
Loan contract, under credit practice rules, 66–67
Loan conversions, 171–72
"Low balance" method, 229

M

Marital status
    and ECOA application processing/evaluation, 96, 98
    request for information of, 94, 139
"Member of the Federal Deposit Insurance Corporation," 77
Metropolitan Statistical Area (MSA), 46, 47, 154, 156, 157
Model Customer Exemption Statement, 25
Monetary instrument recordkeeping requirements, 30
Monetary Instrument Transaction Records, required information, 27–28
Money Laundering and Control Act (MLCA) of 1986, 19
Money Laundering Suppression Act (MLCA) of 1994, 19, 21, 43
Money market deposit account (MMDA), 165–66
Money orders, 113
Mortgage loans, 197
Mortgage portfolio protection plan (MPPP), 149–50
Mortgage servicing, 179–81
Mortgages
    high-rate/high fee, 217–19
    nondepository lenders, 154
    reverse, 96, 219–20
    See also Adjustable rate mortgage rules; Truth in Lending Act (TILA)
Multiple creditors or consumers, 195
Mutual Mortgage Insurance Fund, 161

N

Names on account, ECOA and, 98
NASDAQ, 22–23
National Flood Insurance Program (NFIP), 144–45, 146, 147
National Flood Insurance Reform Act of 1994, 149
National origin, request for information of, 95
Negotiable order of withdrawal (NOW) account, 112, 166
New accounts, 114, 227–28
New York Stock Exchange, 22–23
Night depository, 120
"No cost" loans, 173
"No point" loans, 173
Nonbank financial institution (NBFI), 31
Nondepository institutions, registration of, 43
Nondepository mortgage lenders, 154
Nonsegregated disclosures, 60
Notice of error, 89
NOW account. See Negotiable order of withdrawal (NOW) account

O

Officer of Federal Contract Compliance Programs, 109, 118
"On us" checks, 113–14, 118

$100 rule, 113
Open-end credit, 200
    advertising credit terms, 208
    billing error resolution, 207–08
    cardholder claims and defenses, 207
    cardholder liability, 206
    crediting payments and refunds, 205–06
    definition of, 193
    disclosures. *See* Open-end credit disclosures
    home equity lines of credit (HELCs), 209–12
    issuance of credit cards, 201
    prohibition offsets, 206
    transaction identification, 204–05
Open-end credit disclosures
    additional, 204
    annual percentage rate (APR), 196
    application, 201–02
    finance charge, 197
    home equity lines of credit (HELCs), 209–10
    initial statement, 202–03
    periodic statement, 203–04
    required, 200
    subsequent, 203
    variable rate information, 203, 210
Originator, in funds transfers, 31
Originator's institution
    in funds transfers, 31–33
    payment orders information (travel rule), 33–34
Overdrafts, repeated, 115
Overt discrimination, 92

P

Paid Outside of Closing (P.O.C.), 173
Pass-through accounts, 28–29
Pass-through insurance, 74–76
Passbook savings accounts, 164
Payable through accounts (PTA), 28–29
Payment and loan balance adjustments, 9
Payment changes (ARM), notice of, 10
Payment order information (travel rule), 33–35
Payment orders, 31–33
Payment plans, credit practice rules and, 67
Payments, insurance, 60
Payroll deduction, credit practice rules and, 67
Payroll withdrawals, CTR reporting and, 25
Penalties, disclosure of (CLA), 60
Performance evaluations, CRA, 46, 48, 49–50
Periodic statement disclosures, 82–83
    Truth in Lending Act (TILA), 203–04
    Truth in Savings Act (TISA), 229
Personal identification number (PIN), 201
Point system, 95
Policy Statement on Discrimination in Lending, 138
Postal Service, money orders, 113
Postdated checks, 116
    prohibited practices involving, 133
Poverty levels, and distressed community, 14
Preapproval credit programs, 101

Preauthorized transfer disclosures, 83–84
Premiums on demand deposit accounts, 166–67
Prequalification credit programs, 101
Prescreening, 93, 126–27
    nondiscrimination in, 137
PricewaterhouseCoopers Regulatory Advisory Services, 5
Price WaterhouseCoopers Trust Regulatory Handbook for Financial Institutions, The, 76
Privacy. *See* Right to Financial Privacy Act (RFPA)
Prompt corrective action (PCA) capital category, 75, 76
Property loans, 171
Property, seizure of, 37
Purchase option, disclosure of (CLA), 60
Pyramiding, 68

Q

Qualifying activities as specified by BEA, 13, 14, 15
"Quality of assistance," 92

R

Race, request for information of, 95, 139
Railroad Retirement Board, 185
Real estate. *See* Fair Housing Act; Real Estate Settlement Procedures Act (RESPA)
Real Estate Settlement Procedures Act (RESPA)
    affiliated business arrangements, 178–79
    dealer loans, 172
    disclosures, 179–82
    escrow accounts, 175–76
    escrow statements, 176–77
    fees for required statements, 179
    FHA loan prepayment disclosures, 182
    good faith estimate of settlement costs, 173–74
    identity of person receiving benefit, 179
    introduction and purpose, 171
    laws and regulations references, 182
    mortgage servicing, 179–81
    referral fees and kickbacks, 177–78
    special information booklet, 172–73
    title companies, 179
    transactions covered and not covered, 171–72
    Uniform Settlement Statement (HUD-1 and HUD-1A), 174–75
Realized value, 60–61
Receipts, from electronic terminals, 82
Redeposited checks, 115
Referral fees, 177–78
Refinancing, 194–95
Regulation B, 91, 95, 100, 101, 103, 104, 125
Regulation C, 154, 156
Regulation CC, 112, 114, 116, 118, 121, 229
Regulation DD, 167, 224–25
    disclosures, 227–29, 231
    interim rule amending, 226–27
Regulation E, 80, 86
Regulation Q, 164
Regulation S, 187
Regulation T, 85

Regulation X, 171
Regulation Z, 86, 191, 192–94, 196, 197, 217–20
    See also Truth in Lending Act (TILA)
Regulatory Advisory Services, PricewaterhouseCoopers, 5
Regulatory consumer compliance examination, 4–5
Rehabilitation Act of 1973, 109
Religion, request for information of, 95
Renewed deposits, 75
Report of Foreign Bank and Financial Account Form TDF 90-22.1, 39
Report of International Transportation of Currency or Monetary Instrument, Form 4790, 37
Requests for disclosures, 228
Rescission, consumer right to, 220–22
Residential loans, 136
Residential-related securities, 136
Residual value, 60–61
Retail businesses, CTR reporting and, 25
Retirement accounts, deposit insurance coverage for, 74
Reverse mortgage transactions, 96, 219–20
Right of rescission, 220–22
Right to Financial Privacy Act (RFPA), 30
    agency certification, 184
    bank compliance, 186
    civil liability, 187
    customer notice, 184
    customer notice prohibited, 188
    customer protection, 184
    exceptions to certificate of compliance, 185
    form of request, 185–86
    introduction and purpose, 184
    laws and regulations references, 188
    record-keeping requirements, 186–87
    reimbursement and exceptions, 187
Rollovers, 74

S

Safe harbor, limited, 23
Savings Association Insurance Fund (SAIF), 72
Savings associations, official sign for, 77
Savings (passbook) account, 164
Secondary market transactions, 172
Secondary mortgage market, 136
Secretary of Housing and Urban Development, 103
Securities and Exchange Commission, 23, 193
Security interest
    charges, 216
    credit practice rules and, 66, 67
    disclosure of (CLA), 60
    information, 215
Seizure of property, 37
Separate accounts, ECOA and, 98
Separate maintenance income, request for information of, 94
Service test, 51–52, 55
Servicing, mortgage, 179–81
Settlement costs, good faith estimate of, 173–74
Settlement Costs and You, 172
Sex, request for information of, 94, 139

Signature requirements, ECOA and, 98–99
Signs, required, 76–77
    "Equal Housing Lender" logo & poster, 137, 139
    Truth in Savings Act (TISA), 231
Single ownership accounts, deposit insurance coverage for, 73
Small business loans, 55
Small farm loans, 55
Small-institution performance standards, 50, 53, 55
Social Security Administration, 185
Software. See Computer software & systems
Special Flood Hazard Areas (SFHA), 144, 145, 146, 147–48
Specifically enumerated businesses, CTR reporting and, 25
Spouses
    and ECOA application processing/evaluation, 96–97
    request for information of, 93–94
    signature requirements, 99
Stale dated checks, 115
Standard Flood Hazard Determination Form (FEMA Form 81-93), 146
Stock exchange, 22–23
Stop payment, placed on checks, 115
Strategic-plan evaluation, 50, 53–54, 55
Structuring of transactions, 30–31
Subaccounts, foreign bank, 28
Subsidiaries of listed corporations, 22
Supreme Court, 37
Surety disclosures, 125
Suspicious Activity Report (SAR), 30, 38
Suspicious transactions, reporting of, 30, 38
S.W.I.F.T. system, 34

T

Targeted population, 15
Taxes, disclosure of (CLA), 61
Taxpayer identification number (TIN), 41–42
Temporary financing, 171
Terminal receipt disclosures, 82
Termination, early, disclosure of (CLA), 60
Time account maturities, 228–29
Title companies, 179
Title VII of the Civil Rights Act of 1964, 106–07
Title VIII of the Civil Rights Act of 1968, 146
"Total Annual Loan Cost Rate" table, 219–20
Transaction identification, 204–5
Transfer of funds. See Funds transfer rules
Transportation of currency and monetary instruments (CMIR), 37–38
Travel rule. See Payment order information (travel rule)
Treasury Department. See U.S. Department of Treasury
Trust Regulatory Handbook, The, 3
Trust-related accounts, insurance coverage of, 76
Truth in Lending Act (TILA)
    amendment to, 4, 191
    closed-end credit. See Closed-end credit
    consumer credit, 192
    credit categories, 193
    disclosures. See Truth in Lending Act (TILA) disclosures
    exempt transactions, 192–93

Truth in Lending Act (TILA) *(continued)*
    home equity lines of credit (HELCs), 174, 209–12
    introduction and purpose, 191
    issuance of access devices, 81
    issuance of credit cards, 201
    laws and regulations references, 222
    open-end credit. *See* Open-end credit
    scope of, 191–92
    subsequent events, 194
Truth in Lending Act (TILA) disclosures, 193–94
    annual percentage rate (APR), 194, 195–96
    annual percentage rate (APR) accuracy tolerances, 196–97
    application, 201–2
    calculations and estimates, 194
    closed-end credit. *See* Closed-end credit disclosures
    finance charge, 193, 194, 195, 196, 197–200, 221
    maximum interest rates (ARM), 10
    multiple creditors or consumers, 195
    open-end credit. *See* Open-end credit disclosures
    refinancing, 194–95
    required, 193–94
Truth in Savings Act (TISA)
    account disclosure, 224–29
    advertising, 167, 230–31
    civil liability, 231
    covered accounts, 224
    distribution of disclosures, 227–29
    interest payment, 229
    interim rule amending Regulation DD, 226–27
    introduction and purpose, 224
    laws and regulations references, 231
    periodic statements, 229
Two-day/four-day test, 121

U

Underwriting, nondiscrimination in, 138
Unemployment, and distressed community, 14
Uniform Commercial Code, 31
Uniform Gifts to Minors Act, 74
Uniform Settlement Statement (HUD-1 and HUD-1A), 174–75

U.S. Attorney General, 103
U.S. Criminal Code, 37, 184
U.S. Customs Service, 37, 38
U.S. Department of Housing and Urban Development (HUD)
    Fair Housing Act and, 136, 137
    home-ownership counseling and, 160–61
    Housing and Urban Development Act of 1968, 160
    HUD-1 and HUD-1A, 172, 173, 174–75
    Mutual Mortgage Insurance Fund, 161
    See also Real Estate Settlement Procedures Act (RESPA)
U.S. Department of Justice (DOJ), 93, 136
U.S. Department of Labor, 106, 108, 109
U.S. Department of Treasury, 20, 33, 35
    checks, 113
U.S. Department of Veterans Affairs, 161
U.S. General Accounting Office (GAO), 185
U.S. Postal Service, money orders, 113
U.S. Supreme Court, 37

V

Variable rate information, 203, 210
    disclosures, 203, 210
Veterans Administration (VA), 155
Veterans Administration (VA) mortgage insurance, 145
Veterans Affairs, Department of, 161
Veterans Employment Service, 109
Vietnam Era Veterans Readjustment Act of 1974, 109

W

Wages. *See* Earnings
Waivers, credit practice rules and, 66, 67
"Warrant of attorney," 66
Warranties, disclosure of (CLA), 60
When Your Home is on the Line: What You Should Know about Home Equity Lines of Credit, 172–73
Whole sale purpose institutions, community development test, 52–53
Wire transfers, 33–34